Intimacy Anorexia: The Book

By Douglas Weiss, Ph.D.

INTIMACY ANOREXIA: THE BOOK

Edited by Tiffany Nerguizian
Cover Design by Janelle Evangelides
Interior Design by Jamie Dodd

Dedication

To those on the journey to love and to be loved.

Table of Contents

Intimacy Anorexia: The Book

Introduction

In a hotel boardroom in Dallas, Texas, well over 15 years ago, I sat among some of the leaders in the field of treating sexual addiction. Back then we began to realize that we were seeing something that was quite baffling to all of us.

We were all treating sex addicts professionally and were still early in this new field of sex addiction treatment. We all saw a type of client that we couldn't clinically explain. We characterized the client as male because at the time we were mostly counseling male sex addicts. This hypothetical male client was a sex addict, which usually meant he was habitually having sex with himself, looking at pornography or having sex outside of the marriage.

We noticed however that this man was often not having sex with his wife. This lack of sex lapsed for weeks, months and in some cases over a period of multiple years. This might make sense for a sex addicted client in the midst of his addiction, but these were men in recovery for months or even up to a year or more. Since many of the leaders in our field are also recovering sex addicts, we were looking at this client like "a cow at a new gate," as they would say in Texas. We didn't quite know what to think of it.

It was here we started to discuss a paradigm which would later be called sexual anorexia. Over time, it was clear to me that this dynamic had a whole lot more to do with avoiding intimacy than it had to do with avoiding sex. Now, much later in my career of treating anorexics, very few men and only some women avoid sex. However, both the men and the women were actively avoiding intimacy. Hence, in our field, the terms *sexual anorexia* and *intimacy anorexia* have been used interchangeably.

In your hands is the first book dedicated specifically to intimacy anorexia. This book will be helpful for both the anorexic and the spouse of the anorexic. It has the complement of a workbook which includes more than one hundred exercises and a Twelve Step workbook to promote healing of this unique addiction process that is devastating so many marriages.

You and your spouse deserve true love, intimacy, sexuality, and a relationship that is authentic, fun and full of the hope and dreams you've always wanted. I have seen many brave men and women wage war on this stealth addiction and begin to give and receive intimacy from the love of their lives-their spouse.

You will begin to benefit from the years others traveled before you on this path toward keeping their flawed, but open heart, approachable. You will be challenged; however, there are fewer journeys that are as amazing to watch as a human heart begins to open up toward love.

Happy Trails,

Douglas Weiss, Ph.D.

Intimacy Anorexia: The Book

1

What is it?

I sometimes feel like one who was placed in a culture to observe something before others could. Most of us are no longer old enough to remember the prohibition days of the 1920's in America. What was happening to America in that era was horrible. Alcoholism was running so rampant it was hard to get good employees. Our nation was suffering from alcoholism in every sense but it had no idea what it was then. We had no name for what was happening. The paradigms for alcoholism were many years away.

That's exactly where many of you reading this book may find yourself. You may know something's not right in your marriage. The evidence of coldness, distance, lack of love and connectedness are so prevalent that it almost pushes you to the point of insanity. You're trying to talk to those around you but you can't quite explain it, especially when they see you or your spouse (depending on whom the intimacy anorexic is) as warm and caring. They can't imagine either of you being neglectful of the other spouse.

Pain, silence, withholding and angry outbursts, combined with a sense of hopelessness, cycle in your marriage repeatedly without any significant change. I have had clients go to other therapists for more than a decade and still bang their head against the wall because of a paradigm to explain their situation was not made known to them. Later they discovered the intimacy anorexia information you are about to embark on and they finally felt understood.

Let's go back to our alcoholic friends for a moment. There were two brave souls that decided to swim against the stream in the culture of drunkenness. Bill W. and Dr. Bob decided that they had to stop drinking. Along with some others, Bill W. and Dr. Bob swam against the current, locked hands and hearts, and started a group called Alcoholics Anonymous.

They began to see alcoholism as a disease that needed to be treated. They recognized that some alcoholics had clear similarities to others. Slowly the clergy and clinicians began to look through this new lens as a cultural problem.

As support grew for alcoholics, and having a disease that could be improved, they were becoming living proof that recovery was possible through this new paradigm of alcoholism as a treatable disease. The pursuit of this freedom began by knocking at the door of the medical community of the day. Knock after knock this new paradigm was advancing and over time it was heard.

The medical profession of the day gave way to this new paradigm. Over time, they included alcoholism as a diagnosis and the rest is history. Alcohol treatment became accepted and promoted and millions of people's lives have been changed because of the willingness of a couple of guys that said "no more" to the paradigm that was presently limiting the understanding of their experience.

Recovering alcoholics opened the doors for all addiction recovery programs. Each addiction process seems to start somewhere with a small group, success happens and the knocking begins at the door of the older paradigms. We are at the beginning of a whole new era of recovery as I write these pages. The battles have been fought and won over chemical addiction of every kind and now the battle fronts are on process addictions like: gambling, sex, food anorexia, food overeating, codependency and so many others.

What you hold in your hands is an attempt to be the early formulation of a *withholding* addiction that mostly manifests in marriage. This withholding addiction is called intimacy anorexia. On the following pages of this chapter, I want to walk through the definition of intimacy anorexia.

I mentioned in the introduction how we, as clinicians, were looking at intimacy anorexia. We could see something, but at the time we didn't really have a clear paradigm. Since the beginning of our understanding of sexual addiction, the term "sexual anorexia" was the first tagging of this interpersonal avoidance dynamic that was highlighted in marriage. It didn't seem to fit into any of the current grids of our diagnostic criteria, in our small field or the larger clinical field of psychology.

In this book, we will be including feedback from 21 spouses and anorexics. In reading the stories of anorexics or their spouse, you will clearly see something is going on both inside the individuals and in their marriage. Before I go one step further, I can hear the questions rumbling around in your head, "He keeps talking about inside the marriage. Doesn't intimacy anorexia impact others as well?"

The short answer to that is both yes and no. Marriage is the only relationship that by definition demands emotional, spiritual and sexual intimacy on an exclusive, committed bases over a prolonged period of time, or as the vow goes "to death do us part."

All other relationships can demand some of us, but not all. Even dating relationships can demand all three major aspects but not in a committed or prolonged basis. The back door is easy to find in dating, and harder to find in marriage. That's why intimacy anorexics look normal or even wonderful in the dating process and on the wedding night or a month or so later it's totally different than it was in the dating relationship.

Intimacy anorexia can impact other primary relationships like the children and extended family. However, it's my experience that it is mostly manifested in the marital relationship.

Intimacy Anorexia: Is the active withholding of emotional, spiritual and sexual intimacy from the spouse.

As we continue our journey throughout the book, we will cover various aspects of intimacy anorexia. In future chapters we will even get to the hopeful side of recovery from intimacy anorexia. Firstly, however, I think it would be prudent for us to go more in depth on the definition of intimacy anorexia so that as we move along, and build from here, our definition foundation is strong enough to support the weight of the rest of what we are building.

Active: The first word in the definition of intimacy anorexia is the word, active. The word active is by far the most argued word in the definition of intimacy anorexia by the anorexic themselves. Everyone around the intimacy anorexic agrees that the word active is very appropriate for what they are experiencing. Although it's clear their behaviors of withholding and pushing the spouse away have repeated themselves hundreds or even thousands of times, the intimacy anorexic wants to claim no intention by these behaviors.

I was having a conversation with a telephone client just the other day. I said, "Let's look at another addiction process that doesn't apply to you." He agreed. "Let's talk about an alcoholic who drank for twenty years of his marriage. He would drink, spend money, become abusive verbally and physically to his wife and family, neglecting many responsibilities as a husband and father. Each time he drank, he made a choice to put the bottle in his mouth. Regardless of his family of origin, biochemistry, past abuse or neglect of his own, he chose to drink, do you agree?" "Of course," he said. "So the alcoholic is responsible for his behavior of drinking but you're not responsible for withholding." "Oh, I see," he sheepishly said.

Active means there is a choice. Often there is a clear intention to create pain for their spouse as a byproduct of the anorexic making himself/herself safe, distant or in control. Active means each drink of withholding intimacy from the spouse is an act for which the anorexic is responsible and with recovery can change. The following are responses we received back from surveys completed by anorexics or their spouses on their definition or application of an "active" anorexic .

Todd (Anorexic): *I am pulling away from my spouse and looking for reasons why there should be distance between us. I don't always immediately recognize that I am pulling away. But I do know that after I have done it for awhile and I start asking myself why I don't feel great; I can then recognize that I am disconnected from my wife.*

Pat (Spouse): *My husband has only had sex with me three times in the past eight months yet he is sexual with himself while viewing porn. He denies me affection and has only told me he loves me one time in the past eight months. He rolls his eyes if I ask for a hug or kiss and makes me feel defective if I want or need any form of affection. He is STARVING me emotionally, mentally, physically and spiritually! He denies my hurt if I try to broach the subject saying I'm the one allowing it to hurt me and denies that what is happening is TRULY hurtful. He makes me question my feelings which I know are God given and normal. I am in so much pain!*

Helen (Spouse): *Active anorexia involves surface or superficial connection, connecting on outward/exterior people, places, things (food, friends, and activities). Examples would be: Intentionally staying with others, at other places, to avoid coming home.*

Sam (Anorexic): *Consciously doing a behavior or action with an intended result.*

Titus (Spouse): *Active would be doing one of the behaviors knowingly and willingly.*

Abby (Anorexic): *Now that I know what anorexic behaviors look like both in myself and my spouse, if I choose to continue in those I would be "active." To have the knowledge and not act on it is irresponsible and unloving.*

Stephanie (Spouse): *My husband actively sets out to create situations that avoid being close to me intimately.*

Nancy (Spouse): *He would rather do anything than spend time with me.*

Tanya (an Anorexic): *I am actively anorexic when I sabotage occasions for emotional intimacy by paying more attention to the children, work, housework, television or any other distraction. My husband's anorexia is active when he is dissociated from the events of life that are going on around him.*

Rose (Anorexic): *I am an active participant in anorexic behaviors if I am not working my recovery program. An example of this active behavior is when I consciously or unconsciously make a choice to avoid participating in my life or my marriage.*

Withholding: This part of the definition is quite simple; I have something but I won't (choice) give it to you. An intimacy anorexic has intimacy, actually most intimacy anorexics make great friends, volunteers, coaches, coworkers, just not great intimate spouses prior to recovery.

I have heard hundreds of spouses complain about how the anorexic seems to give intimacy to strangers and friends regularly. It's when they close the door to the world and they're alone that their heart closes and they withhold intentionally what they freely give to others.

I have had spouses jealous of friends because they all get a lot of what the spouse is starving from. Presently, I was talking to a wife of an anorexic and she said, "I just wanted to be treated like a stranger." What she meant by this and I have heard this many times. "You treat others with respect, a smile and are kind to them but you treat me with neglect and criticism." Withholding is, I have a great heart to give but I am not going to come out and play with you and risk getting hurt so I will put you in pain by withholding it from you. This is withholding as an intimacy anorexic.

The following are responses we received back from surveys completed by anorexics or their spouses on their definition or application of *withholding*.

Todd (Anorexic): *Withholding is not providing a connection with my spouse- purposely disconnecting.*

Rachel (Spouse): *We have discussed in detail the importance of touching (this is nonsexual). He always says he will change it, but in reality refuses to, and I know that he can lift his arms and hug someone if he wanted to. I've seen him lift his arms in the air.*

Helen (Spouse): *Keeping to yourself what your spouse wants or needs from you e.g., withholding freedom, withholding friends, withholding intimacy and/or withholding sex.*

Pam (Spouse): *He does not give compliments or apologize for hurting me emotionally. He takes his problems to other women instead of me.*

Virginia (Spouse): *My spouse does not offer, initiate or invite.*

Sam (Anorexic): *Withholding is denying something to another or yourself.*

Titus (Spouse): *Withholding is to not give something like a compliment, a conversation, a kiss hello, a look into the eyes, sex, and any kind of silly playful gestures that may reference sex in any way.*

Monique (Spouse): *Holding back so as to protect oneself from being seen and/or to protect from being hurt.*

Abby (Anorexic): *Similar in my mind to "active," withholding is knowing that something is wanted or expected but keeping that from the person with intent to control or manipulate.*

Stephanie (Spouse): *My husband withholds compliments, praise, affection and joyful times together.*

Allison (Spouse): *Withholding is a way to keep his walls in place.*

Tanya (Anorexic): *One of the ways in which I am anorexic is by withholding love and acceptance when the person I am trying to have a relationship with has disappointed me. My husband is withholding of emotional and sexual intimacy when he perceives that I am rejecting him.*

Miriam (Spouse): *My husband withholds as an active way to express anger and to gain distance from my feelings and his. He does this by staying busy, getting angry, not listening,* and not appreciating. He withholds by not returning to make things right, by saying he "needs to" change/connect/be sexual but then not following through.

Alice (Spouse): Withholding is not connecting with me emotionally. He does not seem to have the ability or does not want to connect in a deep meaningful way.

Rose (Anorexic): I would define withholding as consciously or unconsciously refusing to give or fulfill the apparent needs of my spouse as a result of a variety of emotions I have not resolved. I may withhold praise or certain requests that are within my powers to accomplish just because I am so hurt or angry at my husband I wish to find a way to hurt him back.

Trent (Spouse): Withholding is not initiating any intimacy at all.

Emotions: As humans, we all come equipped with emotions. I know as well as any most of us grew up with very little role modeling or training about identifying and communicating feelings. I, myself, have four degrees and none involved training on how to identify and communicate feelings.

As a clinician treating addictions for more than 20 years, I know that any addiction, whether chemical or process, can limit the emotional development of the person significantly. Even teenagers have feelings. Emotional intimacy, regardless of the skill, says to the spouse, "Here is my heart, flaws and all. I open it as much as I can and behold your heart as well."

Everyone in the real world of relationships knows that pain is part of the relationship process. Emotional intimacy isn't, "I connect, give myself and receive you if you promise never to hurt me, see or mention my flaws or disagree with me." This conditional intimacy and irrational belief for safety in intimacy anorexics will be discussed later in the book. Withholding emotional intimacy says that regardless of how much of my heart I can access and can give to you I won't share my emotional or authentic self with you. This is a choice.

The following are responses we received back from surveys completed by anorexics or their spouses on their definition or application of *emotions* and emotional intimacy.

Todd (Anorexic): *Expressing emotions is being able to identify and verbalize what I am feeling when I feel it and hearing my wife describe what she is feeling when she feels it.*

Pat (Spouse): *My definition of emotional intimacy would be truly sharing himself with me. Any "conversation" he has is surface at best. He is unable to connect with me. He will not answer any of my questions yet demands to know all of my information. He doesn't want to "know me" though. He shames me for wanting a real relationship.*

Marcus (Anorexic): *Application of emotional intimacy is getting emotional support from one's spouse, knowing that they care and support what you are doing to provide for the family.*

Helen (Spouse): *Emotional intimacy is sharing with your spouse true and genuine feelings and thoughts e.g., sharing how you feel about certain situations, or people or your spouse.*

Virginia (Spouse): *Emotional intimacy is being able to describe or share feelings. Sharing the real you.*

Sam (Anorexic): *The application of emotions are the connection where one is open and not protected.*

Claire (Spouse): *Feeling safe to share whatever emotions are present is the application of emtions.*

Titus (Spouse): *Emotional intimacy is when two people are connected spiritually and emotionally to each other in such a way that there is safety when you are with that person. You feel safe and secure with them and can talk about anything without being afraid of how the other will respond.*

Monique (Spouse): *The state of being close to someone to the extent that one can share thoughts, ideas, desires and feelings without fear of being damaged in the process is emotional intimacy.*

Abby (Anorexic): *Emotional intimacy is exposing your true self to your spouse and others without sugar coating your feelings to change their mind. It is the ultimate expression of true love and confident risk. It is standing in the Garden with NO FIG LEAF.*

Claire (Spouse): *Emotional intimacy is when you have a close relationship by supporting each other's needs and you feel secure with your spouse.*

Allison (Spouse): *Being able to share feelings with one another, being honest and not having secrets, being able to accept another's thoughts and feelings without condemnation or feeling threatened or blamed.*

Tanya (Anorexic): *Emotional intimacy is sharing your heart openly and honestly with the person you love.*

Miriam (Spouse): *Emotional intimacy occurs by being genuine with one's own feelings and by having empathy for others. It also means being honest even when it's not easy.*

Alice (Spouse): *Emotional intimacy is letting someone into the deepest parts of your being-not being afraid to be 100% open and honest.*

Rose (Anorexic): *I would define emotional intimacy as emotional, physical and spiritual attention to and from my spouse.*

Trent (Spouse): *Emotional intimacy would mean being able to commend each other or show feelings of affection towards each other.*

Spiritual: The spiritual part of a human being is by far the most intimate part of ourselves. Our spirit is not only the universal place that wants to connect to God; our spirit is a place of knowing, discerning, and having intuition or a sense of things that goes beyond facts.

Spirituality with our spouse is one of the most sacred things on earth. Regardless of the manifestation of worship, prayer, meditation or other connecting rituals, when we share this inner person to our spouse we are sharing our authentic self more purely than merely words can express.

The intimacy anorexic says "No, I'm not letting you into that sacred place." Even the religious intimacy anorexic who will pray with others would rarely pray, worship, read spiritual literature together or just open their spirit up to their spouse. Not allowing the spouse in spiritually is intentional. Again, regardless of skill or background we all have a spirit. Giving the spiritual part of ourselves to our spouse is an important ingredient for intimacy in a marriage.

The following are responses we received back from surveys completed by anorexics or their spouses on their definition or application of *spiritual*.

Todd (Anorexic): *In our spiritual tradition (LDS) it is called "feeling the Spirit." It is those times that I know that I am connected with God. I am willing to do his will. I have spiritual intimacy with my wife when I am able to seek after her joy, ahead of my own, while giving myself permission to join in that joy as well.*

Pat (Spouse): *My husband REFUSES to pray with me, read the Bible with me, or study recovery materials together. My husband has refused to do "Intimacy: A 100 Day Guide to Lasting Relationships" written by Douglas Weiss because it would change all of our lives. We both would have changed, but he does not want there to be balanced and loved in our relationship...he wants me to be controlled and manipulated and for my boundaries to collapse.*

Helen (Spouse): *Sharing with your spouse is spiritual connection. Pouring spiritually into your spouse includes praying with/praying over one another and physically making contact with spiritual intentions.*

Sam (Anorexic): *Spiritual Intimacy is a union with God and openly following His desires.*

Michelle (Spouse): *In marriage, spiritual intimacy means to share in prayer, scripture, and the things of the spirit for example: the treasures of your heart and the struggles, concerns, challenges, and victories. These are woven together with your spouse, whom is or is supposed to be your friend, lover and closest ally.*

Titus (Spouse): *Spiritual intimacy is much like emotional intimacy except that the focus is on your spiritual life. You can pray with each other, read the Bible together, and watch a TV preacher together without feeling fear of being rejected by your spouse...*

Abby (Anorexic): *Spiritual intimacy is being confident and connected with God so that you can be spiritually connected with other believers. True spiritual intimacy, to me, is when I am worshipping God with my spouse and whatever I do or say to the Lord would not be uncomfortable to either one of us.*

Claire (Spouse): *Spiritual intimacy is when you connect on even a higher level.*

Allison (Spouse): *Connecting on a spiritual level through prayer, shared purpose, reading and learning the word, and fellowshipping with other believers.*

Tanya (Anorexic): *Spiritual intimacy is sharing your faith and worship with the person you love without fear of rejection.*

Miriam (Spouse): *To me, spiritual intimacy means being able to connect with God or a higher power and share in this connection with others.*

Rose (Anorexic): *I would define spiritual intimacy with my spouse as sharing regular time in the Word, sharing regular prayer together, sharing regular corporate worship together, and being sensitive to his spiritual needs and vice versa.*

Sexual: Sexual intimacy can be an electrifying intimate event inside a marriage when both spouses are giving and receiving within the sexual encounter. Just as we are emotional and spiritual, we are all sexual. We were sexual from the first slap on the behind at birth until our last breath.

Sexuality is far more than an act; it is part of who we are. Intimacy anorexics can either deny they are sexual or engage as little of themselves as possible in the act of sexuality. The majority of male and female anorexics don't mind the act of sex; it's the giving of their heart or connecting during sex that is scary. The anorexic would say that they'll give you their body, but not their soul or spirit during sex.

This one dimensional sex (physical sex) over time can be unsatisfying for the spouse and an unattractive proposition all together. For some anorexics they purposely negatively reinforce sex so their spouse doesn't want to be sexual with them because of their intentional negative reinforcement.

The other smaller number of intimacy anorexics will have nothing to do with sex. They avoid sex in so many ways by shutting themselves down and over time starve or punish their spouse with their lack of sex that they intentionally create a sexless marriage at the cost of their spouse's happiness. This desire, to be unknown, is intentional. It says, "I won't let you in, no how, no way, no matter what pain I intentionally inflict in your whole being, and too bad for you."

Sexual withholding or sabotaging is a part of the intimacy anorexic pattern for some; it's a primary part for others and for some it's very little of their intimacy anorexia pattern.

Todd (Anorexic): *The connection of our physical bodies after some level of emotional or spiritual intimacy has been achieved.*

Rachel (Spouse): *It should be a beautiful sharing-not the using of a sexual toilet and an emotional sharing-not a biological function like urinating.*

Pat (Spouse): *My husband PREFERS his mistresses, porn, masturbation, solo sex of all forms, fantasy, actual sex with others...sex with anyone besides me...he isn't "with me". As he has admitted, he is not attracted to me and has had to resort to fantasy just to finish the deed with me. He hasn't wanted me in so long and when he is with me I worry he is not with me. I want him to want me and love me. I want to be desired and I am not.*

Marcus (Anorexic): *Being able to have sex without feeling like it is a job for the spouse.*

Helen (Spouse): *Sharing with your spouse your physical body (not just intercourse) e.g., kissing, touching, holding, and intercourse with your spouse.*

Virginia (Spouse): *Being totally engaged in each other...being physically, emotionally and spiritually present.*

Sam (Anorexic): *Being present during sex to experience the act in a non physical way as well.*

Titus (Spouse): *Sexual intimacy is being one with your spouse in a physical way like in love making; you feel safe and want* to give of yourself to them completely unhindered by any negative emotions.

Abby (Anorexic): *Sexual intimacy is when emotional intimacy is firm and practiced, when Spiritual intimacy is growing and deepening and the love expressed by the two create a tri-cord strand.*

Claire (Spouse): *Sexual intimacy is when you're with your spouse; you feel good about yourself, and feel sexy and free to share yourself and do anything to pleasure your spouse.*

Stephanie (Spouse): *I define sexual intimacy as an exchange of touch and then consummation of the loving act while both are attuned to each other's presence and needs. It is a joyful playfulness that brings one closer after the act of lovemaking. It is a bond that grows in wanting to bring pleasure to each other as well as to oneself simultaneously. It is not a dirty act or shameful act or using the other, but rather one where two people exchange the emotions, feelings and bodies in order to gain a higher place. It bonds the love and doesn't make one feel a lack of love.*

Nancy (Spouse): *He will promise me "time" and get everything started, then go off and take care of himself with no explanation.*

Tanya (Anorexic): *Sexual intimacy is sharing the most private parts of your body with the person you love without shame.*

Miriam (Spouse): *Sexual intimacy is a way for two people to take the closeness that develops through being emotionally and spiritually connected to a deeper level. It's a way to connect that allows ultimate vulnerability while being safe and loved.*

Rose (Anorexic): *I would define sexual intimacy as spiritual, physical and emotional connection during sexual intercourse and foreplay.*

Trent (Spouse): *Being felt as "wanted" and "needed" by your spouse to make yourself feel complete.*

Intimacy: Intimacy is the ability for me to let you behold me, flaws and all. I have heard some say intimacy is in-to-me-see. That's clever and I think you get the point. The intimacy anorexic prefers to be regarded as altogether good. Prior to recovery, the intimacy anorexic has great difficulty letting their spouse see their flawed self. Interestingly, as intimacy anorexia progresses over time in a soul they become less able to see the positives in their spouse. It's as if they are (the intimacy anorexic) the good of humanity and their spouse becomes the bad of humanity over time.

It is difficult to be intimate if one spouse is good and the other is bad. Intimacy is, I am flawed and loved and you are flawed and loved. I let you see me, and you let me see you. That's intimacy, and for most intimacy anorexics, they not only say no to this invitation to intimacy, they say, "no way".

Intimacy can be scary for anyone regardless of the gender. For the intimacy anorexic, intimacy can be described as terrifying before recovery. Interestingly enough, intimacy is the only solution for an intimacy anorexic to recover.

Spouse: As we mentioned earlier, there is something about marriage that demands what the anorexic wants to withhold, and that is long term emotional, spiritual and sexual intimacy. Even a marriage with healthy people can be challenging at times.

We all experience pain, rejection, anger, disappointment and the whole gammit of emotions inside a marriage. If you are an intimacy anorexic you recoil from this type of pain within a relationship...then the dance of anorexia begins. The anorexic recoils or pushes the spouse away and the spouse has to create ways of dealing with this to try to get intimacy from someone who is actively withholding it.

The anorexic applies a variety of strategies to create or maintain distance in this relationship. This distance allows the intimacy anorexic to feel safe, protected, in control and is not going to be threatened by genuine intimacy. The strategies anorexics use differ from couple to couple, as to what is effective to create distance. However, over time, you can see anorexic strategies build a fortress toward their spouse.

The spouse really is the primary target of the addiction to the withholding process. Others will be impacted either directly or indirectly by this addiction to withholding; however, the person with the most consequences from intimacy anorexia is the spouse.

I have seen amazing courage displayed by both intimacy anorexics and their spouse. The spouse can be a man or woman who has written a huge check to keep the marriage together throughout the years of being blamed and vilified. When intimacy anorexia has been clearly identified and they accept full responsibility for their withholding behaviors this can dramatically change both of their lives.

Love and intimacy are possible. If I had not seen changed people and changed marriages over the decades, I would not write one word of this book. I have seen miracles of recovery from many addiction processes including intimacy anorexia.

The intimacy anorexic who chooses recovery can positively affect their life and the lives of those they love. So, keep reading. Regardless of the past damage done, by the intimacy anorexic, if there is effort and willingness in their soul, then recovery can happen.

Intimacy Anorexia: The Book

2

Characteristics

After our dialogue about defining intimacy anorexia, we are now at a point where we need to be even more specific in what we are talking about. So far you have heard me use the term *withholding* as if it were related to intimacy anorexia. Now, I want to discuss what particular behaviors are indicative of intimacy anorexia.

To eye these behaviors independently, here and there, or to observe a few would not give you the ability to understand intimacy anorexia. That's what is so helpful about having a clear paradigm. With a clear paradigm you will be able to piece A, B and C together as an end product and live life accordingly. This can be no truer than with the paradigm of intimacy anorexia. Here, I am going to lay out ten specific characteristics of intimacy anorexia. I'll also throw in an extra one just for fun that I often hear from my clients or their spouses.

As you read through this chapter, if you are the anorexic, try to keep your heart and mind open. If you're not sure if one applies to you, then ask your spouse. He or she would most likely be able to give you a clear picture from their perspective. As in any list of characteristics, you won't necessarily have all ten, but you or your spouse may have enough characteristics to still qualify for being an intimacy anorexic.

Busy

The first characteristic of an intimacy anorexic is *being so busy you have little time for the spouse*. This is a really common characteristic of most intimacy anorexics. This doesn't mean that the spouse is traveling all the time, although that could definitely be a way to avoid intimacy. Let me give you the more subtle ways in which a spouse is able to keep themselves busy so they have little time for their spouse. I will break this down into two categories: inside the house and outside the house.

Let's start with inside the house. An intimacy anorexic keeps so busy that they have little time for their spouse. First we'll discuss those that have nothing to do with technology, then those that are technology based. One way to stay busy is always doing housework e.g., cleaning this, that, and rearranging regularly. Children also bring several ways to avoid the spouse. This may include: doing homework together with a child, without the spouse or playing with the children and excluding the spouse or having projects around the house. I know some anorexic couples that buy and live in fixer-uppers and they are constantly doing projects and have no time for each other.

There are the readers who avoid through the newspaper, latest novel, or self-help book or writers who endlessly write instead of relating. Then there are those who need to sleep so much that they avoid connecting with their spouse.

Technology is a dream for intimacy anorexics, since it can feel as if they are actually doing something or even relating to the images on some type of screen. The computer, and especially the internet, is the greatest avoidant strategy. The anorexic may be involved in social networking, shopping, checking weather, chat rooms, pornography, games, gambling, research, etc. This may take up hours while their spouse is in the other room waiting to relate.

There is older technology that is another terrific device, that allows you even to be in the same room as your spouse, even next to each other, and not relate. That's right; I'm talking about the television. That device should be called the intimacy zapper. You're both in altered states, separated from each other and when you do come back to reality, you are then too tired to talk. By the time you pry yourself off of the furniture it's time to go to bed.

Computer games and video games are also a way for anorexics to distract themselves from their spouse. These games have become very realistic. Saving a false world from destruction, for example, is often more valuable than connecting to the one you said you would love, honor and cherish. In house avoidance, strategies need to be addressed or avoided for recovery from intimacy anorexia.

Some intimacy anorexics have busy avoidant strategies to actively withhold intimacy from their spouse. These activities can also be very positive and easily justified by the intimacy anorexic. The person who volunteers to avoid intimacy has a cause they are helping and can justify their absences. The religious person is saving the world, but intentionally withholding from their spouse. The over worker avoids intimacy while justifying their behavior through work to create more money. Then there is the golfer, sports participant or sports fan who is loyal to themselves and a team but isn't intimate with their spouse.

"Busy" can take so many forms it could be a book all by itself. Any of these behaviors could be fine in a marriage if they are staying connected to their spouse. In the absence of connecting, "busy" becomes a way which the intimacy anorexic actually withholds intimacy or even the potential for intimacy through this type of avoidance. Below are responses from intimacy anorexics or their spouses about the characteristic, busy.

Rachel (Spouse): *His "busy" includes work, his hobbies, his brother, his counseling...anything!*

Abby (Anorexic): *Busy, was just an excuse. Priorities were really messed up, such as, not spending quality time with my husband, and not putting him first. The kids and their needs took over and there was no balance. It became easy for me to "fill my day" with activities so I was exhausted and would fall asleep early with no energy e.g., cleaning, cooking, doing school activities, church and Sunday school.*

Helen (Spouse): *My ex-husband was a truck driver. He intentionally took jobs over the road to stay away from home.*

Todd (Anorexic): *Watching TV late at night, being exhausted at the end of the day from all the work that I did, going to scouts or church meetings were my "busy".*

Virginia (Spouse): *My husband keeps so busy and forgets to spend time with me and so I can blame him for that part of our relationship or for acting in on his addiction. He doesn't remember special days or holidays.*

Sam (Anorexic): *I go to work early instead of cuddling in the morning.*

Titus (Spouse): *Busy, is never saying no to anyone but your spouse. Your spouse will have a hard time (or a complete inability) telling people no. She ends up being too busy all the time and never has time for the relationship.*

Rose (Anorexic): *I would define busy as being emotionally, physically or spiritually unavailable for relationship with my spouse on a regular basis. I would define this business as a repetitive pattern that is not due to physical handicap or illness, but is purposeful avoidance of relationship.*

Monique (Spouse): *My husband is always "working" and needing to finish things before he can leave his office and/or come to bed. This has caused a lot of damage to our physical relationship as well as to our emotional closeness, because it affects the amount of time we can talk together. It has affected his relationship with our children as well because of the many times he said he would "be right there" and then never came.*

Claire (Spouse): *My husband is so busy at work that when he gets home he is too tired physically and mentally to even want to have sex.*

Stephanie (Spouse): *As the spouse I see how every spare moment my husband has away from his job is dedicated to being busy; Lawn/yard work, fishing hunting, chopping wood, fixing everything, and gardening. Then when he comes in at night from these non-stop chores, he just collapses for the night on the couch watching TV. Doesn't matter what is on, even nonsense, he just has to watch it. He could be doing things to improve himself, our marriage, our intimacy but he always chooses to put it LAST.*

Nancy (Spouse): *He starts getting romantic, then goes off and spends three hours on his palm pilot.*

Allison (Spouse): *His busy includes: TV, computer, paper, anything to distract him from just being with me.*

Alice (Spouse): *My spouse stays busy with outside business, relatives, and friends so that he does not have time to connect with me or communicate with me on any meaningful level. There's just not enough time for that.*

Blame

Blame, as an anorexic characteristic, is almost universal. Blame, as a characteristic, is *when an issue or problem comes up in the marriage; the anorexic blames or puts responsibility on the spouse for the issue, before they can see their contribution to the problem or issue.* As you understand anorexia better and how an intimacy anorexic wants to be in the "good box" all of the time, it makes being flawed, irresponsible, thoughtless, careless, and bad less desirable to discuss (if you are the anorexic).

Blaming is almost reflexive for many anorexics. I am absolutely amazed at how much the emotional survival of the anorexic is at stake, if they are found to be flawed, like the rest of us. Often they can't be honest about their intentional withholding. Starving their spouse directly affects the behavior they receive back from their spouse. Below is more feedback from anorexics and their spouses about the characteristic, blame.

Rachel (Spouse): *He'll say I'm too fat, but I'm the same as when he met me.*

Helen (Spouse): *Blame is mentally manipulating to stay hidden from yourself or being exposed.*

Todd (Anorexic): *Starting a fight with my wife, being upset that she hasn't cleaned the house enough, being upset that she is behind on school work, being upset at her wanting to ask me questions are all my excuses for blaming her.*

Holly (Spouse): *My spouse will blame my weight gain as a deterrent to sexual intimacy.*

Marcus (Anorexic): *If life is going wrong it is always the spouse's fault.*

Abby (Anorexic): *If he didn't work so much, if he didn't drink, if we had more time...it was all about him. I blamed him for not being the spiritual head of our household, for not wanting to go to church, for not going to church and setting a bad example for the kids...then I blamed myself for not being able to make him do those things!*

Titus (Spouse): *Blame is when you are in communication, not meant to be confrontational, but it is perceived as an attack. The spouse lists all of the reasons why it is your fault for the situation. My wife and I try to talk about our lack of a sex life and somehow by the end of the conversation it is basically all my fault once again. She will tell me it's not me; it's that she just has no desire for sex. But if we have not made love for several weeks and I get upset about it she will tell me that the reason she doesn't want anything to do with me is because of my being upset.*

Claire (Spouse): *My husband was sexually abused when he was a child and I know that is a good part of the problem. He also works a lot and has a lot of responsibilities at work so he comes home very tired and mentally unavailable. He says he's tired, work is aggravating him, it's always excuses, yet he blames me for not wanting to have sex. Even if we are on vacation and the weather is perfect and we are staying at a great place having fun, he is still not in the mood.*

Tanya (Anorexic): *I have used his sex addiction as an excuse to blame him for my emotional withholding.*

Stephanie (Spouse): *My husband holds in his emotions and feelings but his behavior shows his anger and blame. He blames me for his lack of wanting to be intimate or the fact that I have made it such an issue. However, I truly have only brought it up about once a month because I have needs and I did not see him making any effort. It is like he enjoys having a hate/need relationship with me. He finds ways to blame me so that he can remain angry at me thus not get too warm and close.*

Allison (Spouse): *I get told, "I never tell you anything because of how you react." When I would try to talk to him about sex and why we never have it, he would say it was because of something I did or did not do. If there was an increase in sexual activity, and I would ask him why, he would say it was because I was being nice to him; I didn't think I was being any different.*

Rose (Anorexic): *I would define blame as using my spouse's behavior as a reason to accuse him of something he was not responsible for instead of looking at my own behaviors. Blame includes displaced anger and failure to take responsibility for my own behavior.*

Alice (Spouse): *My spouse blames me for everything that goes wrong. He uses me as an excuse for his acting out. In his mind, he convinces himself that I "nag" at him all of the time. In actuality, that is not the case at all.*

Withholding Love

The anorexic often has a difficult time perceiving the intangible nature of withholding love. To withhold love is *to not give to your spouse love the way you know to or how they have asked to be loved.* Each one of us wants to be loved and yet we all experience being loved in many different ways. Spouses may want emotional sharing, long walks, a thoughtful note or gift that says "I was thinking of you." Some just want help around the house or with the children. However, your spouse needs to be shown love and the anorexic already knows how the spouse wants to be loved.

Here is how to know what type of love your spouse needs and if you are withholding that from him/her. The anorexic convinces their spouse that they love them in the way they receive love. This leads to the decision to marry you. If you go back to dating, what meant a lot to him or her? Secondly, when you really get in trouble in your marriage or the marriage is threatened, what do you do to make up to show you care? Lastly, if your life was dependant on your answer, could you say how your spouse feels your love the most? If you're the intimacy anorexic, and you agree now that you know how your spouse receives love, then why are they doing without it? If you don't have a clear rational reason, without blaming, then let me suggest that you are actively, intentionally withholding love from your spouse. Below is feedback from anorexics, or their spouses, and what they have to share about withholding love.

Pat (Spouse): *My husband can't say he loves me...as a matter of fact he doesn't know if he does. I've been married to him for almost two years and I am disposable. I am worth nothing to him.*

Holly (Spouse): *Love is intellectually accepted but not emotionally felt.*

Sam (Anorexic): *Opening the car door for her every time and never being appreciated.*

Abby (Anorexic): *Not getting the love tank filled, lack of joy and celebration is withholding of love and is a slow fade. It is a game that I wish I never played. Tit for tat...kind of like sex...if I am not getting it from him, then I will get it from somewhere. So my love tank was filled with friends, my children, family, activities, things I excelled at like work and running marathons.*

Titus (Spouse): *A few weeks back my brother-in-law and his kids were living with us, one afternoon we both arrived home at exactly the same time and were walking up to the house when my wife came out and greeted her brother put her arm around him and walked him into the house, leaving* me standing there as if I were invisible. That was a very hurtful experience. Later I ask her about it and she had no idea, and even denied that even happened.

Stephanie (Spouse): *Deep down within my husband's limited emotional grasp of what love is about, I believe that he feels he loves me. I feel he just needs me and that almost anyone would fit the role he has me in. I am the wife who keeps the house together, provides his meals, picks up his dry cleaning, and makes conversation with others when we are at some function. I contribute to the community, his shield and cover, yet I am also the one who rubs his head, neck and back. I make sure he takes his vitamins, prescriptions and eats right. I laugh at his jokes but he never laughs at mine. He thinks I will never leave because of my religious beliefs and he knows I will never have an affair. But, I am seriously on the line thinking it is time to leave because this has greatly affected my physical health.*

Nancy (Spouse): *He can't find a phone at work to let me know he is working late.*

Allison (Spouse): *I wrote a book, a whole novel; I worked on it for years and it was a goal of mine to finish it before I turned 40. I did; he never asked to read one page.*

Rose (Anorexic): *I would define love as a choice to direct my intimate, physical, spiritual and emotional needs to one person only, my spouse.*

Withholding Praise

The withholding of praise is also a significantly recurring behavior for intimacy anorexics. To withhold praise is *to not share with your spouse about their positive qualities as a person and their positive impact on your life.* Let's go back to, "if your life depended on it...". If you had to write ten things that are amazing and positive about your spouse or how he or she is impacting your life in a positive way, my bet is again, you could absolutely make a list pretty quickly.

If you're an anorexic, think about the last week or month and how frequently you intentionally praised your spouse. How often are you praising your spouse in front of their family, your friends or even the children? If you're the spouse of an anorexic, reflect on this as well. When was the last time you really received a heartfelt praise without asking for it from your spouse?

All of us have amazing, positive qualities. Anorexia, over time, closes this positive vision and tends to focus on the flaws of the spouse. So, if you haven't been praising your spouse regularly for who they are and all they do, may I suggest that you could be actively and intentionally not praising them? Below are some comments from anorexics and their spouses about the characteristic of withholding praise.

Rachel (Spouse): *He thinks praise is telling you, "supper is great". It is letting you know what that you look pretty or that you are sexually attractive to him.*

Helen (Spouse): *Building up and affirming someone is praise.*

Todd (Anorexic): *When my wife is specifically seeking to ask for praise on something she has done well, I will usually just say very little or in a tone that really downplays the obvious effort she has taken.*

Pam (Spouse): *There is no praise from him and has not been for more than four years.*

Holly (Spouse): *Praise is given only when asked for.*

Marcus (Anorexic): *Telling her more times how pretty she is or just letting her know that I am glad to have her in my life.*

Titus (Spouse): *I recently asked my wife why she never compliments me anymore, and since then she has been trying but it doesn't come naturally for her. She will usually give me a compliment once I have complimented her first.*

Tanya (Anorexic): *Praise is outwardly acknowledging the attributes of my spouse that I appreciate. This is very difficult for me when his addiction or anorexia is rising up. I punish by withholding praise.*

Nancy (Spouse): *He comes home to a room that is freshly painted and wallpapered and finds the one spot where the paper doesn't meet perfectly. I made his favorite chocolate cake a thousand times and he always found something wrong with it. His sister made it once and he praised her all night.*

Allison (Spouse): *I got my masters degree and I never received even a card.*

Rose (Anorexic): *I would define praise as verbal, physical or spiritual reinforcement that my spouse finds valuable.*

Alice (Spouse): *My spouse is unable to see the good in me or praise me. He chooses not to praise me for anything because he wants to keep control of me and tries to make me think that everything is my fault.*

Withholding Sex

By far, of all the behaviors that are characteristics of intimacy anorexia, withholding of sex is probably the easiest to measure, and at the very least, most obvious. *Withholding sex from your spouse is avoiding having sex, sabotaging sexual encounters or not connecting emotionally during sex.* You can tell whether you are the spouse or the anorexic by observing the last time you had sex. It might not be as easy for the anorexic to remember the last time he or she sabotaged a sexual encounter, whether it was before, during, or after the encounter. It is even harder for the anorexic to remember withholding emotionally and spiritually during sex or really giving all of themselves to their spouse. Any of these behaviors can be withholding sex. In the intimacy anorexia workbook, I give some of these examples:

- During sex, do you look at your spouse or close your eyes?
- Do you think of other things to do during sex?
- Do you fantasize about others or porn during sex?
- Do you communicate positively during sex?
- Are you silent during sex?
- Do you act as if you dread sex?
- Do you hurry your spouse to get it over with?
- Do you leave your spouse emotionally or physically after sex?
- Do you shut your spouse down when talking aboutsex?

Below are comments from intimacy anorexics and spouse's of anorexics regarding withholding sex:

Rachel (Spouse): *Ha ha! This is a joke right? This is anorexic behavior. It doesn't exist.*

Todd (Anorexic): *My wife will specifically ask to have sex with me and I will turn her down for one reason or another. Usually I will find some reason that I am angry at her as the reason not to have sex or make sure that I am too busy.*

Pam (Spouse): *The sex was all about satisfying him-no emotion involved, only physical for his relief.*

Holly (Spouse): *There is no sex and all talk of sex is cause for a subject change.*

Abby (Anorexic): *I always thought of sex as a way he affirmed his love for me. It was all about love and devotion. I thought he was proving by connecting sexually that I was the one. I remember one time that he told me it would be nice if I were to initiate sex once in a while...I always thought I did. Couldn't he read my mind? Once again the communication, the sharing of time and emotion was not there so the sex was lacking.*

Titus (Spouse): *Sex is seldom and when it is, she has to initiate because I gave up trying years ago. When we do have sex, most of the time she is completely detached from the whole experience which makes it unfulfilling. Every once in a while (maybe two or three times a year) she will engage emotionally and it is the best sex ever.*

Monique (Spouse): *During our separation, we have come to a place of almost no physical relationship. I find it difficult* to relate to my husband on a physical level because my emotional needs are not being met. He wants physical closeness to get emotional closeness, and I want emotional closeness before I can give physically.

Nancy (Spouse): He promised to take me out and spend an evening of romance and gets as far as pouring the wine, then goes over and spends three hours talking to a neighbor he never talked to before.

Allison (Spouse): Sometimes weeks, sometimes months, would go by without sex and he was mostly blaming me for us not having sex. I was always ready because I figured I had to take what I could get.

Miriam (Spouse): My husband has many fears, excuses, repeated promises for "later" that never occur. He makes promises to me and to our therapist to engage in sensual activities that he doesn't do. He occasionally offers to "have sex" (service me). He doesn't notice me as a woman and doesn't engage in flirtation or foreplay. He literally turns away from me when I'm dressing or undressing.

Alice (Spouse): My spouse has sex with me more out of responsibility than out of anything else. He tries to avoid any kind of meaningful connection.

Withholding Spiritually

The characteristic of withholding spiritually also is only noticed by the spouse. I have had clients that were spiritual leaders, pastors, rabbis, and even medicine men that didn't connect spiritually with their spouse. Withholding spiritually is *withholding spiritual connectedness from your spouse*. This mean regardless of faith practices or lack thereof there is no real spiritual connecting behavior with the spouse. The anorexic might be religious to the hilt, but spiritually not authentic in the presence of their spouse.

I've heard countless excuses especially from the religious (regardless of faith) anorexic. *I do this just by myself. It's not my personality. My spouse is too spiritual (or not spiritual enough) so I don't connect with them spiritually.* Regardless of the rationalization there is an absence of spiritual connecting between the intimacy anorexic and their spouse. Below are examples shared by anorexics and their spouses regarding the lack of spiritual connectedness they have experienced.

Ted (Anorexic): *I will go to bed instead of reading scriptures or praying together. I know that if I do those things, sex usually follows afterward.*

Pam (Spouse): *We don't talk about spiritual things because he does not want to know what I believe.*

Virginia (Spouse): *My spouse will say a 20 second prayer with me at bed time. He will not pray with me otherwise, attend Bible study or talk about God. He does not lead or offer any spiritual offerings to my children or me.*

Michelle (Spouse): *Sometimes I will pray with him, but mostly I don't, as it's difficult to do so with a person I cannot trust or feel safe around.*

Titus (Spouse): *I lead different small group studies from time to time or even a prayer gathering and she will seldom want to be a part of it.*

Tanya (Anorexic): *We don't pray together other than at meals and bedtime. My relationship with God is so special that I fear sharing it with my husband, because I don't want him to sabotage it.*

Feelings

This characteristic can be described as *being unwilling or unable to share feelings with their spouse.* Having difficulty sharing feelings is also a universal characteristic of the intimacy anorexic. As we stated earlier, addictions hinder emotional development.

If you're the spouse of an intimacy anorexic, you may have difficulty remembering a time that your husband or wife voluntarily shared feelings with you without having to write the "emotional check" for the experience. If the anorexic's image of the marriage is threatened or he or she really blows it somehow, you can expect some feelings being shared but soon fades away again within a week or two after the activating event.

The sharing of feelings is an act of authenticity that can be scary, difficult or both for the intimacy anorexic. Their unwillingness or inability to share feelings can be intentional so as to not give you love the way they know you like it. There is a time when it could legitimately be a skill deficit and in that case when he or she does the Feelings Exercise with you, you will both experience real effort and connecting. While doing the Feeling Exercise, if the anorexic is not trying to connect, but appears to be checking off a box, you will experience the "unwilling" part of this addiction to withholding.

Below are more experiences about feelings from both anorexics and their spouses.

Rachel (Spouse): *Feelings, I have them all and he has none. Not true, he has passion for cars, guns, machinery-you know, the important things (HIS STUFF)!*

Pat (Spouse): *I am not allowed to have feelings and if I do express them they are invalidated by him. He does not honestly share with me. He strives to keep me feeling crazy. He refuses to tell me what he really wants-marriage or divorce. I have no clue what he really wants.*

Ted (Anorexic): *I work really hard to not show when I am crying. I will usually not talk about my feelings.*

Holly (Spouse): *My spouse's feelings are always unknown.*

Titus (Spouse): *My wife doesn't even know how she feels most of the time unless she is angry, which is her most common emotion. When we talk she will not look at me and she likes to play solitaire on her phone while we are in a discussion.*

Claire (Spouse): *My feelings have been hurt terribly and my husband doesn't care about my feelings. It's like he's saying my feelings don't matter to him or that I'm not important enough to him to work on this problem.*

Tanya (Anorexic): *After stuffing my feelings for decades, it has been very difficult to thaw out my emotions and truly feel life. I have learned through recovery to acknowledge my feelings and accept them for what they are.*

Nancy (Spouse): *If I want to know how he feels about something, I have to listen to him talk to his mom on the phone.*

Allison (Spouse): *He told me last summer, that I liked to go deep and he just liked to not think about things and just have fun. He will not share anything with me about how he feels. If I ask him, he gets angry and starts to blame and accuse.*

Criticism

Having ongoing or ungrounded criticism which leads to distance in the marriage is the seventh characteristic of intimacy anorexia. This can be the low grade put downs toward the spouse, noticing what they do wrong, or just regularly pointing out their bad ideas.

The ungrounded criticism has little to do with reality. That strategy may be to push the spouse away or throw them off the trail of something, either way it's intentionally creating distance.

Criticism in this category does not need to be spoken. So many spouses have told me that their husband or wife doesn't actually speak their criticism but they can feel it constantly.

If criticism is an active strategy, the intimacy anorexic will be much faster at making a list of what's wrong, defective or weak about their spouse than what is amazing. Criticism can also be employed in a binge tactic to push away, when intimacy or sex could be expected. This would include: birthdays, holidays and right before vacations. This is the intimacy anorexic pushing the spouse away so they don't have to give emotionally or sexually to the spouse. Below are some comments from intimacy anorexics and their spouses about the characteristic of criticism.

Rachel (Spouse): *Not so overt, just a general sense that I will never be good enough for him compared to the fantasy world he lives in. There is nothing I can do to compete in this world. We were driving down the road one day getting water to spray the crops. I was having a good day and was happy to see him and was chatting exuberantly about many things. We were about to drive by a house where a woman was out in her front lawn in a bikini. He just stared at her and couldn't hear a word I was saying. I felt like someone had kicked me in the stomach and then I thought I was imagining it. So when we came back the other way I watched to see his reaction. Needless to say I was not wrong and he went so far as to turn and look at her a couple times and then smiled and waved at her. How friendly, NOT! He never looks at me like he looked at her and he didn't even know I existed. I feel constantly compared and I just don't measure up.*

Todd (Anorexic): *I find something that she is not doing well around the house and use that as the reason that I am upset.*

Pam (Spouse): *I don't dress right, talk right, think right, kiss right.*

Holly (Spouse): *My spouse criticizes as a means of creating distance between us.*

Marcus (Anorexic): *I always try to find something that I can criticize her about if there is conflict.*

Sam (Anorexic): *I make sarcastic remarks so I am not directly putting someone down.*

Titus (Spouse): *There are those days that I drive too slowly, too fast, and pick the wrong parking space; I feel as if I can do nothing right.*

Tanya (Anorexic): *I can be hypercritical of people around me if I don't feel that they are living up to my standards, and I punish them with rejection.*

Rose (Anorexic): *I would define criticism as belittling behavior, verbal or physical toward the other spouse. It is usually very personal and intended to wound, harm, discourage, control, beat down and destroy my spouse's spirit.*

Anger/Silence

My experience with intimacy anorexics is that not all use silence or anger as a characteristic of their intimacy anorexia. However, those that use anger or silence as a characteristic use it with a vengeance. This intimacy anorexia characteristic can be described as *any use of anger or silence to push away, punish or control the spouse.*

I have countless hours listening to stories from spouses and intimacy anorexics alike about the employment of using anger or silence toward their spouse. Sometimes the examples are extreme, including times when the intimacy anorexic wont' talk to his or her spouse for days or weeks while living in the same house. The anger explosion is often over something minor and is a great tool to push the spouse away and avoid giving their hearts to them.

If the intimacy anorexic uses anger or silence as a tool, in their anorexia, you can expect it often. If the intimacy anorexic chooses to recovery, this behavior will need consequences and boundaries to conquer. This characteristic is best explained by real life examples such as those listed below from intimacy anorexics and their spouses.

Pat (Spouse): *I am punished by silence. I have had some anger since the affair, before I never expressed it. I am not allowed to express even a hint of dissatisfaction or disagreement with my husband. If I do, he accuses me of fighting. He gives me the silent treatment. He seeks to control me that way. I feel cursed by Eve that my desire is for my husband and he has no desire for me-that he can be so cruel and selfish and not feel any guilt or remorse for breaking my heart repeatedly. He accuses me of punishing him. I believe it is the other way around. I feel punished for loving and trusting him, for trying to be a good wife, for wanting to please him, he has rewarded me for these things with extreme abuses and cruelty.*

Helen (Spouse): *He uses intentional aggression or shutting down verbally to push away.*

Todd (Anorexic): *I will do this whenever she is getting too close to me. I will start playing the blame game and get angry at her or stop talking to her.*

Holly (Spouse): *Being an anger addict, my spouse intimidates me to control me.*

Claire (Spouse): *Unless things at work and in family are "just right," we all walk on eggshells.*

Sam (Anorexic): *When I am losing an argument, I clam up and just offer an abrupt agreement to end the discussion.*

Abby (Anorexic): *I use silence first and then it erupts into explosive anger at random times. Silence is something I have had lots a practice with in my family of origin. Children are to be seen and not heard. Silence for me is very tied to feelings e.g., keep it in, don't feel, don't talk. Anger is a result of that. Sometimes the anger/silent combo can be done at once. Where I am not saying anything with words, but my actions, body language and spirit tell another story.*

Titus (Spouse): *When we are in a heated discussion she will often just get up and leave the room and refuse to talk anymore, sometimes she will not say anything to me for a couple of days or until I reach out to her and apologize.*

Monique (Spouse): *My husband is angry with everyone right now. He is angry with his counselor and is refusing to do the homework he has been assigned. He has not seen his counselor in almost five months because of this. He is angry and critical with our children for not helping him in the office. He is angry with me for asking him to leave and for not letting him come back yet. He has thrown temper tantrums; if it wasn't so serious, I would laugh at how comical it looks for a grown man to be swinging his arms and legs like a two year-old.*

Tanya (Anorexic): *I have often used rage or silence to control those around me. If my loved ones don't act the way I believe they should, I punish through anger, shame and silence.*

Stephanie (Spouse): *If he doesn't like something I ask or do, he just turns me off for a long time. He just gets cold and claims nothing is wrong. It is rare he will talk it through.*

Nancy (Spouse): *He stopped talking to me for about two years and wouldn't even answer a question about the kids.*

Allison (Spouse): *He watches TV without comment, expression or emotion and falls asleep by 8:00 or 9:00 p.m. every night. He gets angry if I try to get close to push through his walls.*

Rose (Anorexic): *I would define anger as rage, shaming behavior, physical violence, sexual violence, isolation, curtness directed toward the other spouse with the intent to wound, harm, discourage, control, beat down, break and destroy the spirit.*

Miriam (Spouse): *Anger is always his primary expression. He occasionally works to get below it but more often than not, he looks for excuses to get/stay angry. Anger is his security blanket.*

Money

The characteristic of *controlling or shaming the spouse about money issues* is probably the least common among intimacy anorexics. Those that employ it, use it with an iron fist. Most of the anorexics who control or shame with money do so by keeping the spouse ignorant of the finances, give their spouse an allowance, make the spouse ask for money, and won't allow the spouse to have a credit card or check book.

However, there is the other side of controlling through money as well. I call it controlling through abundance. This spouse, male or female, has substantial money but controls with it. Their attitude is, I buy you everything so don't complain about a lack of intimacy, love, or sex. This type of controlling by money isn't as obvious as those that control by not giving.

Shaming the spouse about money can also be a part of this intimacy anorexic characteristic. In this case it's perfectly okay for the intimacy anorexic to spend money on whatever they like but the spouse has to account for everything or is put down for purchases, even legitimate ones. Below are some examples of this characteristic from intimacy anorexics and their spouses.

Rachel (Spouse): *He expects me to pay for most things when my income is limited. I have started to refuse. We don't do much anymore.*

Todd (Anorexic): *I will not watch our finances for awhile. When it gets scary enough, I will tell my wife that we can't spend any more money which disproportionally affects her and what she needs to buy for the family, more than it affects me.*

Tanya (Anorexic): *I do not feel I am anorexic with money. My husband is more anorexic with money. There is always money to spend on what he wants, but he nags about expenses for the home or kids. He especially nags about leaving lights on.*

Nancy (Spouse): *If I ask for anything, he'll say I spend all of his check before he gets it. He never says no to the kids or his family. He will spend $200 on pizza and bowling with them, but returns hamburger to the store if I spent $.20 too much. He never lets me buy "wasteful" things like paper plates or disposable diapers. He spends more on lunch for himself and his buddies from work than he gives me to buy food for the whole family.*

Allison (Spouse): *We eventually had to have separate checking accounts and divided the bills and paid them on our own. It was the only way we could function. We could never discuss and come to an agreement on any money issue. It was always me having to submit to him.*

Rose (Anorexic): *I would define money as any finances between spouses. Financial control can involve withholding towards spouse or overindulgence toward self.*

FREE

Remember at the beginning of the chapter I said I would throw in a free characteristic. Well, here it is. The keyword would be "roommate." *The spouse of the anorexic feels like or has stated feeling like a roommate.* I have heard this same comment so many times from spouses that I add it to the end of my assessment oftentimes as I am assessing clients for anorexia.

Congratulations, you have gathered a lot of information in this chapter. Below I have listed the ten characteristics again. There are three ways to respond. A characteristic is listed along with a place to respond with "Y" or "N" for yes or no. First, respond as you see your behavior and secondly as your spouse might see your behavior (assuming you are the anorexic) and thirdly your spouse's actual response.

Characteristic	As I'd Respond	As I think Spouse Would Respond	My Spouse's Response
Busy	(Y) N	(Y) N	Y (N)
Blame	(Y) N	Y (N)	(Y) N
Withholding Love	(Y)(N)	(Y) N	(Y) N
Withholding	(Y) N	(Y) N	(Y) N

Praise

Withholding Sex	(Y) N	Y N	(Y) N
Withholding Spirituality	(Y) N	Y (N)	(Y) N
Feelings	(Y) N	Y (N)	Y (N)
Criticism	(Y) N	Y (N)	Y (N)
Anger/Silence	(Y) N	Y (N)	Y (N)
Money	Y (N)	(Y) N	(Y) N

If you have five or more "yes" responses to these characteristics, I would encourage you to keep reading; you are most likely an intimacy anorexic. If you have much more than five "yes" responses, then you definitely have the right book in your hands.

If you are the spouse and you see your spouse or yourself or both of you in these characteristics, I would also encourage you to keep reading. Remember, there is always hope for those who are willing and able, to apply the effort, to change.

3

Causes

In any discussion on addiction, there is usually a natural pause taken to ask the legitimate question as to how this happened. Regularly, couples that are dealing with the insanity of an addiction process that they have no paradigm of explaining, travel to my office to attend a Three Day Couple Intensive. They are often toward the end of their emotional resources, as their heads have been swirling for years, trying to figure out if one or both of them are crazy, codependent or they simply just don't know what to think. After assessing one or both with intimacy anorexia, the clouds begin to clear and at least we have a paradigm of understanding what we are dealing with, and so they begin to feel hopeful.

Shortly after their feelings of hope, one spouse will lean toward me slightly and say, "Doc, how did I (or my spouse) get this way?" It's a sincere and legitimate question that I want to take some time to answer. We'll walk through the primary causes of intimacy anorexia that I have observed in my twenty years of counseling clients with this issue.

Cause #1 Sexual Trauma

Sexual trauma is at the root of many addiction and mental disorders. It is one's sexuality being ravaged, shamed and damaged by strangers, friends or family members. Whether it is one time or hundreds of times by one or more person(s), it creates pain for the entire being of its victim. This pain will have to be addressed by the soul in some manner.

Let me tell you a true story that happened to me as I was working on my masters degree and working in the chemical addictions unit at a large psychiatric hospital. I will call the patient Mike for our story. Of course, that's not his real name.

There was a time long, long ago, before insurance companies had managed health care, that an alcoholic with insurance could stay in an inpatient treatment center for 90 days or longer. At this time, I was in grad school working on my Master's degree. One of my jobs was driving the alcoholics and drug addicted patients from the psychiatric hospital to their Twelve Step meetings.

Mike was about 40 years old and a raging alcoholic. Mike was motivated during his stay at the hospital. He would go to therapy, Twelve Step groups, read his recovery literature and over a short time became "Mr. Recovery." He would do well while in the hospital and most of the staff were sad to see him leave.

Mike would leave and then "it" would happen, he would get so pathetically drunk he would have to admit himself back into the hospital. This happened to Mike three times. That meant Mike was in the hospital more than not over a course of a year. Over that year, I became certified as an alcohol and drug abuse counselor. So as Mike came back to the hospital for the fourth time, I was assigned to do his assessment after he detoxed.

Mike and I sat in the little room not much bigger than a closet. We were going over his drinking history. As we did, I said to Mike, "I could fill this out without you; I know you so well." Then I had a clinical intuition moment and I said, "Mike, is it okay if I ask you a question that is not on the intake?" He said, "Sure Doug." I asked Mike, "Have you been sexually abused?"

You could have heard a pin drop and I am sure Mike's heart was just pounding. He looked down to the floor then back into my eyes and said, "Yes, when I was 12, 13, 16, and 19, all by men, twice at gunpoint, and one with a knife to my throat." I said, "Have you ever dealt with this issue?" What he said I will never forget, "Not sober."

You see, Mike had untreated sexual abuse. Although he could get sober, he couldn't stay sober. Many men and women with addictions have experienced sexual trauma. I don't want to get graphic here, so as not to trigger someone, but the pain of the sexual trauma needs to be addressed by the soul.

There are things that were held true by the victim before the trauma such as: the world is a safe place, people are safe, and I can trust. These beliefs about the world, others and trust are shattered when someone is sexually abused. The survival of trauma has to create a world view that now fits their experience. These traumas often happen early in the development of the victim of sexual trauma. They occur early enough in the development of the victim that they often do not yet possess abstract reasoning. This is the reason that the victim will often blame themselves or at least believe that they are fatally flawed because of the event.

It's here, where decisions and agreements with your own heart and its safety, have to be made. The intimacy anorexic, as a result of trauma, can clearly make the decision that they are not safe, and their heart and body are not safe. The decision to not allow that pain to happen again e.g., no risk, no vulnerability, are actually normal and age appropriate decisions to survive such a vicious trauma.

The decision to survive by shutting down their heart can lead to consequences for decades. The survivor now has an opportunity to carry out the decisions and agreements they made for survival, but these decisions can limit them when the time and opportunity comes to truly live.

During the time of survival, the victim of sexual trauma can mitigate this pain in so many ways that are totally unpredictable. They create structures to protect themselves that later can easily morph into an intimacy anorexia structure.

Sexual trauma is when one person (the perpetrator) uses the victim as a sex object. Being used as an object can clearly set up the survivor of abuse to relate to others and themselves as an object which is one of the chapters we will get into later. At this point it's enough to say that when one relates to themselves and others as objects, they become limited in relating to people as souls. You could see how marriage could be difficult if someone primarily relates to people as objects and not as souls.

Simply put, the abuse survivor survives the abuse and is now protecting themselves and relating to others as objects. They are most likely married to someone who needs intimacy but they already made an agreement to themselves that they could never give again and feel safe. This dynamic I just described is at the core of some of the intimacy anorexics.

Fortunately, if an intimacy anorexic has experienced sexual trauma, they can seek and receive help. They don't want to be defined by their perpetrator's acts and beliefs. We can't choose be free of abuse; however, we can choose to do the work to reclaim our soul to be able to give and receive love again.

Cause #2 Attachment Issues with the Opposite Gender Parent

Addicts of all kinds share, for the most, part some family of origin issues. Here, I am not trying to place blame, but rather share with you a cause for intimacy anorexia that I have seen with many.

If you are a man, the opposite gender parent is your mother. If you are a woman, your dad is the opposite gender parent. These opposite gender relationships are the first and primary relationships where you experienced and generalized about the opposite sex. This is a normal process we all go through.

If your mother is cheerful, spiritual or depressed you could easily think all women are the same way. If dad is handy with tools, respectful, angry and selfish you could easily generalize these characteristics about men.

Let me share with you three patterns I have heard intimacy anorexics experience from their cross gender parent. The first pattern of the cross gender parent that I have heard quite regularly is the opposite gender parent is not safe.

This parent might be shaming, tell their child's confidences to others, be unpredictably moody, angry, drunk or mentally ill in some way. The young soul can't predict safety at any time with this parent. They, over a period of time, conclude their heart is not safe in this relationship with their opposite gender parent. Remember these experiences are happening early in a child's life. It is really not a far leap to say to yourself at this age that you'll never trust a person (gender) like that again. The child then locks into a survival mode with agreements that will keep them from intimacy in their marriage.

The second type of parental experience from the opposite gender parent is the distant and emotionally unavailable parent. They might have been home every night and drove you to band practice, but there was no intimacy, no relating, often not being heard and feeling unknown by this parent. The heart of this child tries for awhile but concludes that this parent doesn't want to know them and concludes that their heart staying open to this parent is not only unsafe, but unnoticed and the child eventually agrees also to close his or her heart to survive the neglect of this opposite gender parent.

The last pattern I see with the cross gender parent is, total abandonment. Abandonment might not be intentional; it could be through the death of a parent. Abandonment can also be intentional, a dad who abandons his teenage girl who is pregnant, a divorce where a parent is not involved after the divorce, a parent who cheats on their spouse and now doesn't want anything to do with the former family, or a spouse with a mental disorder who leaves or commits suicide.

Each child longs for attachment to their biological parents. This longing doesn't change because of circumstances or the irresponsibility of the parent. The child's heart can choose to close and conclude that there is no reason to keep their heart open since it's only going to be abandoned anyway.

Cause #3 Sexual Addiction

Sexual addiction is an often seen cause for intimacy anorexia, especially for men. The sex addiction empowers the anorexia and the anorexia empowers the sex addiction. Sex addiction is when someone uses sex in a way to medicate or deal with life. They have tried to stop and often have a secret sexual world from their spouse. It is common for sex addicts to be intimacy anorexics.

In a journal article I wrote called *Sexual Anorexia: A New Paradigm for Hyposexual Desire Disorder,* I discuss that men who stated that they were sex addicts, 29% of them scored high enough to also be intimacy anorexics. The females that identified themselves as a sex addict had a 39% chance of also being an intimacy anorexic. The wife of a sex addict was also at a 39% chance of being a sexual anorexic.

If you believe that you or your spouse may be a sex addict, take this short test to start that dialogue. Below, answer "yes" or "no" to these ten questions.

1. Have you had sexual behaviors you wish youcould stop?

2. Do you feel abnormally driven by your sexual drive?

3. Have you been in relationships just for sex?

4. Has masturbation been ongoing even after marriage?

5. Has pornography continued for you even after marriage?

6. Does your sexuality seem to be dragging down your personal potential?

7. Do you find that you spend a significant amount of time online, viewing pornography or grooming others for sexual encounters?

8. Have you experienced an unwanted sexual encounter during childhood or adolescence?

9. Has monogamous sex grown to be boring?

10. Have you tried to stop some sexual behavior and failed repeatedly?

If you answered yes to five questions, you may be a sex addict.

6 Types

If you have identified yourself or someone else as a sex addict, it's important to know what type of sex addict. In my book *The Final Freedom* and *Addicted to Adultery,* I discussed the six types of sex addicts. If you believe that you or your spouse is a sex addict you can visit the website www.sexaddict.com and take the Six Types Test.

If sex addiction is part of the picture for your situation seek help immediately. An intimacy anorexic who is a sex addict, male or female, cannot heal from intimacy anorexia unless the sex addiction is treated. Below are the six types of sex addicts.

The Biological Sex Addict

The Biological Sex Addict has attached his or her sexual reward system to fantasy, porn or an object. Their reward system has conditioned them to the point that it is seeking a high chemical reward to continue to attach to the object of desire.

Almost all sex addicts have the biological type of sex addiction. In my clinical experience, I would say about 15 percent of the sex addicts I have treated are only biological sex addicts. The purely biological sex addict is the easiest to treat and most likely to be successful in recovery.

The Psychological Sex Addict

This sex addict has suffered some type of emotional, physical, spiritual and moral abuse or neglect. The abused person has a clear understanding of what has occurred, because it was obviously a violation and, in many cases, an ongoing violation. Those that have been neglected or abandoned often take a little more work to see the pain and its impact in their life. Most are less aware of their past neglect, because it is difficult to miss what you didn't have.

The Spiritual-Based Sex Addict

The spiritually-based sex addict is a person who is filling their spiritual void or what we call the "God hole" with sex. I love doing a particular exercise with a spiritually based sex addict. I ask them to describe the characteristics of God to me. They will usually rattle off several characteristics, such as loving, accepting, always available, there when you really need help, strong and nonjudgmental. Then, I have them give me a list of the characteristics of the addiction or their "boo boo mommy" (their fantasy girl). They generally reply with caring, loving, accepting, fun, unconditional love and non-critical.

Every time I do this exercise, it's blatantly obvious to the spiritually-based sex addicted client that their sex addiction is a replacement for authentic spirituality. For this type of sex addict, their addiction is their religion. It's where they worship, offer themselves and gain a sense of transcendence, peace and tranquility. As odd as it may seem, the addiction is their spirituality, even for some who have a faith. Pragmatically, they go to the addiction for help in times of trouble.

Trauma-Based Sex Addict

The trauma-based sex addict is someone who has experienced a sexual trauma. Although 80 percent of sex addicts are sexual abuse victims, not all are trauma-based sex addicts. The sex addict who is trauma based is an addict who is specifically reenacting their sexual trauma. Let me give you two illustrations to help you understand this type of sex addict.

Randy is a successful business man and in a committed relationship. Randy, however, is a sex addict. He is cheating regularly. Randy discovers on the Internet that he is a sex addict. He wants help with his sex addiction. During his assessment, I ask about early sexual encounters. When Randy was about 14 years old, he went into a car with a stranger where an adult man sexually abused him. Then, two weeks later, he was in a public bathroom, and an adult man sexually abused him in the bathroom. Randy didn't tell anyone and repeatedly masturbated to these sexual abuse encounters.

Now, Randy could be having anonymous encounters or affairs anywhere all the time, but guess where 95 percent of his acting-out encounters occurred? That's right, 95 percent of his sexual encounters were happening in cars and public bathrooms, two very confining areas to be sexual. His acting out was a direct reenactment of his sexual trauma. Randy had never seen the correlation and was able to do the work to disconnect from the trauma and stop the addiction to anonymous encounters.

Bart was a 42-year-old man, significantly overweight and depressed. Actually, so depressed he was suicidal. He was admitted to a local hospital for his suicidal issues. His psychiatrist wanted me to do a sexual assessment on him. I arrived at the hospital, and we sat in a small room where I asked him why he was there. He said he wanted to kill himself, and I asked why. Bart said very straight faced, "I am having sex with nine women outside of my marriage, and I can't keep up with it anymore."

At this point, I understood why the psychiatrist ordered the sexual assessment. When I went through Bart's sexual history, he told me about his first sexual encounter. Bart was 14 years old, when he went down the street to play with his friend. His friend wasn't home, but his friend's mom asked him to come in, and she gave him oral sex. A couple of days later, they had intercourse. He and this woman had sex 2 to 3 times a week until the week before his wedding at 35 years old. For almost 20 years, Bart was sexually abused.

I asked him to describe the various other women he was having sex with outside of marriage. All the women were 15 to 20 years older than him. He was duplicating his sexual trauma exactly.

The trauma-based sex addict is stuck in the trauma. Bart could have acted out with young women, strangers or prostitutes, but because of his trauma, only a much older woman could satiate his addiction.

Intimacy Anorexic Sex Addict

The intimacy anorexic sex addict is a man or woman who has both addiction processes going simultaneously. They addictively withhold from the spouse and addictively act out sexually with fantasy, masturbating with pornography or various sex acts with others. This person has to address both addictions to be successful at recovery from either addiction.

If the sex addict is also anorexic and this is not treated, relapses in sex addiction are almost certain. In most cases, the withholding (anorexia) is the primary addiction and sex addiction is secondary. The intimacy anorexic sex addict often needs professional help to heal both the addict and the spouse of the addict in order to repair the marriage. I would definitely recommend a Three Day Intensive if this is your situation.

The Sex Addict with Mood Disorder

In a past journal article I wrote, *The Prevalence of Depression in Male Sex Addicts Residing in the United States,* I discovered 29 percent of male sex addicts struggle with depression. It can be that the depression occurred first, and the addict was using sex to medicate the depression, or that the addiction and its consequences were causing the depression.

Another common mood disorder I see in my office is Cyclothymic Disorder. In my clinical experience, about 15 percent of addicts have this mood disorder. Cyclothymic Disorder can be defined as a mild "up" for several days and then an unexplainable "down" day one or more times a week. Bipolar disorder and/or manic depressive disorders can also be present. These disorders have higher ups and downs and are often longer in duration. You can go online to obtain specific symptoms of each disorder.

A mood disorder for the sex addict has a chemical imbalance neurologically of some type. The sex addict with a chemical imbalance then treats the symptoms of the imbalance with a sexual release in adolescence and it continues on if recovery is not sought. The habit of medicating the imbalance through orgasms creates a sex addiction pattern. This chemical imbalance, if not diagnosed, can also set in motion influences that can create a desire to act out sexually, even if the addict is trying to get sober.

Cause #4 Role Modeling Neglect

This is by far the lesser seen cause for intimacy anorexia but I have seen it reoccur in my assessment of intimacy anorexics. I have heard both male and female clients state they felt they were managed more than parented.

A child can feel managed in a situation where an older couple has a child out of duty but really didn't want the child or in a large family where there is no connecting to the parents. Another example is the anorexic couple that got pregnant one of the rare times they had sex.

A child whose parent(s) has intimacy anorexia and saw no care toward each other nor any real connectedness or closeness can become anorexic. He or she grew up with no connection so not connecting is normal. They grew up where a child was not to be seen or heard.

I know one man who practically raised himself. He would have a key to let himself into the house and went to bed while rarely seeing his parents at all during the week for years. Aloneness becomes expected and normal. This neglect can also produce generalizations about relationships in the child that can lead toward creating an intimacy anorexia structure to survive.

For some intimacy anorexics, they have only one cause that was a major contribution on their road to the addiction of withholding. It's not uncommon for someone who is an intimacy anorexic to have more than one cause for the anorexia structure to grow in their life.

Regardless of the cause, there is hope if someone really wants to work at their recovery and has a willing spouse to do their exercises with when it is safe to do so. Each start of the journey to becoming an intimacy anorexic is unique. You have your own story of becoming an intimacy anorexic. At some point as you work through the workbooks for intimacy anorexia you can put many of these pieces together and start to move along a different road-the road to recovery.

I hope this discussion on the causes of intimacy anorexia was helpful. I hope this chapter leaves you with three important ideas. The first idea is that there may be legitimate reasons for the intimacy anorexic to have closed his or her heart a long time ago. Secondly, I hope you realize you did not cause the intimacy anorexia to occur in your spouse. In most cases the factors that were in place happened prior to marrying you. Thirdly, there is hope, if the intimacy anorexic does the recovery work, to have a marriage much better than it has been.

4

Initiating Anorexic Patterns

"What in the world makes my spouse act like this Dr. Doug? I'm going crazy with this…," an animated spouse was expressing to me. He wasn't asking what caused it, such as our previous chapter's discussion. He was sincerely asking what ignites this otherwise normally functioning person to randomly shut down and withhold a whole list of things.

I have heard all kinds of colorful reiterations of the same question regarding what ignites this blizzard of coldness toward the spouse. In this chapter, I will outline several igniters of the anorexic behaviors. Each intimacy anorexic has their own primary pattern that causes the choice to actively withhold from the spouse. Here are the major igniters of the anorexic behaviors.

1. Avoiding Intimacy

Let's go back to the definition of intimacy anorexia; it's the active withholding of emotional, spiritual and sexual intimacy. If things are going along really well, and the intimacy anorexic is feeling close to you and feeling like an intimate, emotional, spiritual or sexual encounter is about to occur e.g., the children are all at grandmas, and there's anticipation of real connection or a sexual rendezvous, this could ignite an anorexic withholding behavior or several behaviors to occur. This withholding or pushing away is intentional, to give the spouse pain so they won't want intimacy or even want to ask to be close to them. When you see an acceleration of anorexic behaviors, back up and see if the two of you were getting close. If you track this, it may be an igniter of intimacy anorexia patterns.

2. Safety

One thing many intimacy anorexics talk about is safety. Many of them have bought some fantasy that they are not to be hurt or questioned. They really want safety, not most of the time, but all of the time. If they feel unsafe, even if they simply make it up that they are not safe, this could ignite an anorexic pattern of behavior.

Usually if this is the stimulation to choose withholding, you can expect the really big guns to come out. The big guns are the ones that hurt the spouse the most. If safety is the issue, expect a grenade, not just an emotional bullet.

3. Fear of Being Flawed

If you're not anorexic this one won't make sense at all. We, as humans, are all flawed. We expect we will be ignorant, make mistakes, hurt others, embarrass ourselves and at times be caught or exposed when this happens. Trying to live in the "I'm really good" box and being found out to be flawed, can ignite an anorexic pattern of behavior.

I have noticed regularly that this can work in one of two ways. First, the anorexic does something less than wonderful, they know it, and they know it will probably be noticed. Here they will employ the active withholding or pushing away strategies to divert attention from the soon incoming data that they are flawed.

Secondly, if the spouse is questioning the anorexic, and is getting pretty obvious that they are flawed, by making a mistake or not planning thoroughly, you are headed for a road bomb and if you get too close it will blow up with so many anorexic behaviors at one time it can become very painful to you.

4. Control

The non-anorexic person realizes that there is little control in their lives. They don't really believe they control people in their life when they can barely control themselves well. They have no faith in the illusion of control or even controlling the perception others might have of them. Really that's just way too much work for most of us.

The intimacy anorexic on the other hand really believes in control for the most part; controlling others, their image, and how others might perceive them. So if control is threatened by circumstances, changes of schedules, or just reality, this can ignite an intimacy anorexic pattern of behavior. You see when you are in control you don't have to be authentic, close, connected or much of anything and will decide how much of yourself you will give to your spouse (control). If an intimacy anorexic is feeling the illusion of control slipping they might exert intentional withholding behavior in attempt to balance themselves.

5. Not the Fantasy Object

Remember that intimacy anorexics often live in an object world. The relational world is often too dangerous for the intimacy anorexic to reside in for too long. In the object world you can exchange characteristics like you would order extra features on an automobile.

One particular day you might not be the right object. You might not be rich enough, helpful enough, or a certain personality or physique. You are simply not the right object for the day. Since you are not doing it for them you can be punished. This entitlement to the right object upon demand can trigger an intimacy anorexic pattern of behavior.

If you're the spouse, you didn't do anything wrong and changing won't get you loved. They might be triggered by a picture in their mind about almost anything that could make them happier. At that moment you are not the fantasy object. If you're the spouse this one can drive you crazy because it can be so random and you would have no clue. However, if you get a dose of random anorexia you could be in the middle of an anorexic storm you didn't create.

6. Stress

Regardless of what the addiction is, stress can activate its usage. It doesn't matter if the addiction is alcohol or shopping, stress is an agent that can bring the addiction patterns to be expressed.

In this case it will be very easy to see when the anorexic patterns get activated due to a particular situation. These situations would be different for each individual. For some, it's stressors from their family of origin. For others, it's their own children, the stress of work or just simply financial stress. Addicts are prone to activate around stress. If you see this in yourself, you'll need to address this in recovery.

7. A Way Not to Acknowledge They Are Sexual

This is really simple, to avoid having sex the anorexic will activate any and all withholding patterns to pull away or push the spouse away. For some, avoiding sex is the most important agenda. Anything that will cause the spouse to be queued into that they are sexual or want to be sexual will get an immediate anorexic response. There's no way they are going to accept the reality that they are sexual. Sex is normal to desire. The fact that they are intentionally creating pain for their spouse and that they really they don't care demonstrates that their sexual avoidance is much more important to them than giving of themselves sexually.

These intimacy anorexic behaviors will mostly come up prior to sex, but if they lost that battle, sometimes you can expect the emotional exiting or grenade during or after sex too.

8. Commitment to Distance

Like a puppy that's been abused or neglected some anorexics will activate anorexic patterns when they feel their bubble is being encroached upon. They have a commitment to distance. They know exactly how far they can be pushed to be authentic or connecting. If that line is crossed, the spouse needs to be punished to reestablish the distance between the two of you.

This commitment to distance is real and if you try to break it you will pay. If you're the spouse and this activates the anorexic patterns you probably have a pretty clear history of this happening regularly. If you're the anorexic, you might need to think honestly if you have a commitment to distance that needs to be addressed as you move toward recovery from intimacy anorexia.

5

Is it an Addiction?

I counsel with sexually addicted clients and their spouses quite a bit in my office. As we discussed earlier, the prevalence of this population having intimacy anorexia is close to 30-40%. This high prevalence demands that I assess both the husband and wife for intimacy anorexia if they are coming in for sex addiction recovery.

Well, you can imagine the eye opener it is for them when I discover one or both has intimacy anorexia as well. This is especially true when the sex addicted husband has cheated on her and she finds out she also has an addiction. She is addicted to withholding. It's also a surprise to many sex addicts that they don't have just one addiction but two. They are addicted to withholding from their spouse as well as acting out sexually with themselves or others.

Unlike the ugly or sloppy addictions like drugs, alcohol or sex, intimacy anorexia is stealth, unseen until detected by usually someone else. The immediate defense is I don't have an addiction, my spouse does. "I'm not sick, they are" is a classic denial defense mechanism I usually have to work through on day one of my Three Day Couple Intensive.

Within the following pages we are going to take a look at the qualifiers of an addiction. These qualifiers would apply regardless if you were a workaholic, shopaholic, alcoholic or an intimacy anorexic. Read each qualifier with an open mind and see if any or several of these addiction qualifiers apply to the intimacy anorexic in your marriage.

1. Efforts to Stop

In this qualifier the addict has come to a place, whether internally or externally, to get motivated, to apply effort, or to try to stop an addictive behavior. This is a moment of clarity for the addict when they realize that what they are doing isn't working anymore and they begin to make some effort to stop the addictive behavior.

These rational moments can be due to an internal crisis from the pain they are in or a realization of the pain they are creating for themselves. More often these low moments are externally stimulated by their spouse due to the spouse's pain. Maybe the addict losses a job, a lover, a spouse or has some legal or financial problem due to their anorexic behavior and momentarily he or she tries to stop the addictive behavior.

Most intimacy anorexics have also experienced a bottom moment, such as: "'I wish my marriage was better,' 'I wish I could show them the love I feel,' 'I want to want sex,' 'It's wrong what I am doing to my spouse-he is a good person and deserves better.'" These statements would be internal bottom moments.

These external moments are also very likely to occur to the addict that withholds from their spouse. This could be defined as the spouse's crisis where he or she is becoming irrational with anger, sobbing because of the months, years or decades of rejection. Most likely there were many long nights that were spent arguing about the unmet needs that have been clearly and repeatedly communicated. Eventually the spouse threatens to leave or they are served with divorce papers. The painful moments in the life of the spouse become external moments that can help the anorexic reach a bottom realization of their addiction to withholding.

After such an event there is some effort to love, connect or have sex to show that the anorexic can change. The effort is real and might even be sustained for days or weeks. Inevitably though, failure of the sustained closeness or connectedness occurs. Inevitably the same withholding behavior occurs again, and the withholding behavior is fully in place until the next bottom moment.

Any intimacy anorexic, with the help of their spouse, could see a pattern where some effort was made; however, it was followed with repeated failure to sustain intimacy. There is a space for you to check off, both as the anorexic and the spouse, which of the ten anorexic behaviors apply. If you've seen this behavior, tried with effort to control it, but failed, circle Y.

	Intimacy Anorexic		Spouse	
Busy	Y	N	Y	N
Blame	Y	N	Y	N
Withholding Love	Y	N	Y	N
Withholding Praise	Y	N	Y	N
Withholding Sex	Y	N	Y	N
Withholding Spirituality	Y	N	Y	N
Feelings	Y	N	Y	N
Criticism	Y	N	Y	N
Anger/Silence	Y	N	Y	N
Money	Y	N	Y	N

Below are some comments from anorexics and spouses of anorexics. These comments can help illustrate efforts an anorexic has had at attempting to stop anorexic behaviors and not being successful.

Rachel (Spouse): *I have been as honest as possible about what I expect and how I feel about things. I have read countless books and websites and tried to give him time, space, and the materials to read. I have cried, reasoned, begged and pleaded.*

Pat (Spouse): *I saw my spouse try briefly after I learned of the affair, ONLY BRIEFLY, to stop withholding affection. But it was always, "Hasn't it been long enough?" I think there were brief moments he tried. But he didn't understand, because he treated having to have a relationship with me as a punishment to him. I was punishment to him; it hurts to even type that.*

Sam (Spouse): *Because of the past affairs, I will not have physical sex if he will not wear a condom. I am not sure I am able to have sex, emotionally or spiritually either.*

Titus (Spouse): *My wife and I have been in marriage counseling that I pretty much forced her to attend, but this whole subject of emotional or sexual anorexia never came up. And although there has been improvement in some areas, our relationship is a real struggle.*

Claire (Spouse): *My husband will call me and say, this weekend we'll go out to dinner and a movie if you want to and he'll be more attentive. He'll give me a massage, hold my hand more, but still no sex.*

Stephanie (Spouse): *My husband has sought professional help but to no avail. He does not complete anything. He procrastinates and then resents me if I inquire about the progress.*

Miriam (Spouse): *After days/weeks apart, he will apologize, reconnect, and promise to change. There have been some periods of real closeness and connection at times, but eventually I want to become sexually intimate, and he becomes passively and then actively angry and withdrawn.*

2. Read My Lips

This was a classic political line in the George Bush election. He looked straight in the camera and made a promise not to raise taxes. As time and circumstances changed, he did exactly what he promised in his campaign, not to do, negating his famous campaign line of "read my lips."

In politics, we expect broken promises; that seems to be the norm. Similarly, in addiction, there is also a norm of not keeping promises. The addict promises their parents, probation officer, boss, lover, sibling or almost anybody that they are going to stop whatever it is they are addicted to. Sometimes these promises are just internal. They say to themselves after something painful or humiliating has occurred, "I need to stop." Sometimes they just look in the mirror the morning after looking themselves straight in the eye and say, "That's the last time. I am never doing that again."

Promises are made to others as well and not kept. The addictive behavior continues days, weeks or months later. Hence there is a promise, sometimes sincere, to stop a behavior; however, the promise is void because the addiction behavior repeats.

For the intimacy anorexic the internal promises sound like, "I really need to try." "I'm not going to do that anymore." "I'm going to enjoy sex." "I am going to be more caring, connecting, sensitive, and positive." By the way, they sincerely mean this each time they promised it to themselves.

The external promises of an intimacy anorexic goes something like, "I'll try harder." "I will stop squandering time on the computer, watching television, volunteering so much, or spending so much time on the phone." "I will date more, not work so late, have sex more often, and not go to bed before you come home."

These promises are often after a conflict or confrontation of the spouse's pain. The intimacy anorexic absolutely means to keep that promise and might, but short term. However, they have the "read my lips" problem and revert back to their withholding days, weeks or months later. In the below space, circle the box "Y" that apply to the intimacy anorexic making promises to quit a behavior and then failing to do so. A line is provided for the spouse and intimacy anorexic to answer these separately.

	Intimacy Anorexic		Spouse	
Busy	Y	N	Y	N
Blame	Y	N	Y	N
Withholding Love	Y	N	Y	N
Withholding Praise	Y	N	Y	N
Withholding Sex	Y	N	Y	N
Withholding Spirituality	Y	N	Y	N
Feelings	Y	N	Y	N

Criticism	Y	N		Y	N
Anger/Silence	Y	N		Y	N
Money	Y	N		Y	N

Below are some comments from anorexics and spouses of anorexics. These comments can help illustrate the broken promises of an anorexic.

Rachel (Spouse): *Every time we discuss what is happening he will say, "This has to change" and the next day it is the same thing.*

Virginia (Spouse): *My spouse says he loves me and will treat me better but gets angry if I say we haven't spent any time together.*

Holly (Spouse): *Promises are no longer given significance because my anorexic spouse breaks them.*

Tanya (Anorexic): *I made promises that I would be more affectionate and caring. That would last for a while, but it wasn't a real change.*

Michelle (Spouse): *So many times he made promises, but now he virtually states he's never had a problem, and it's me instead.*

Titus (Spouse): *My wife will not make a promise, but she will say I want things to get better and then will not do anything in any concrete way to make a change.*

Claire (Spouse): *My husband says he'll go for counseling and either will never make the appointment or he will only go 2 or 3 times and then stop. I've stopped trying. There is nothing I can do now to make it change and I have now lost all hope. I keep thinking that when the reasons he would use like the kids, work, being too tired, gets a different job, or gets the position he wants, no longer pertained, I had hoped that then it would be better. But they all have come and gone and no changes so no hope anymore.*

Stephanie (Spouse): *He has promised many things. I have found recent evidence he even lies to the professionals. I am tired. I have surrendered. I have disengaged from the dance.*

Rose (Anorexic): *Consequences I have had because of intimacy anorexia have included much retribution behavior to punish my spouse which actually backfired and made him angrier. Consequences have also included hours, weeks and days of mutual isolation from each other.*

3. Consequences

Every addiction has consequences. The consequences can be a smashed car, broken relationships, or a smeared reputation. All types of things can happen as the addict tightens their grip on the addiction and loses their grip on reality.

Consequences for the intimacy anorexic are sometimes actually the end game of intimacy anorexia. The spouse that used to be full of life is now critical, depressed and angry most of the time. The absolute distance in the relationship is a consequence. Not having sex or kindness in the relationship is also a consequence of intimacy anorexia.

Sleeping in different rooms is a consequence (again this might be intentional). Like the alcoholic who is drunk doesn't necessarily feel the pain of the consequences, so is the intimacy anorexia who is drunk with withholding and avoidance behaviors. In the below space identify if there have been consequences due to the acting in or withholding of a particular anorexic behavior.

	Intimacy Anorexic		Spouse	
Busy	Y	N	Y	N
Blame	Y	N	Y	N
Withholding Love	Y	N	Y	N
Withholding Praise	Y	N	Y	N
Withholding Sex	Y	N	Y	N
Withholding Spirituality	Y	N	Y	N
Feelings	Y	N	Y	N
Criticism	Y	N	Y	N
Anger/Silence	Y	N	Y	N
Money	Y	N	Y	N

Here are some comments from anorexics and spouses of anorexics. These comments can help illustrate the consequences of anorexic behaviors.

Rachel (Spouse): *I feel that my mental, emotional, spiritual and sexual well being has been seriously damaged.*

Todd (Anorexic): *Increased tension in my marriage. When I am in my anorexic phase, I am much more desirous to act out sexually. Loss of self esteem.*

Virginia (Spouse): *A lonely marriage. Many activities we are invited to, we don't attend or I attend by myself.*

Tanya (Anorexic): *The main consequence that I have suffered from my anorexia is the distance I have put between me and those I love. I do not have the loving relationships that I desire because of my fear of being hurt and rejected. I have pushed away those I love, and put walls between us.*

Claire (Spouse): *I started questioning myself as though something was wrong with me. Am I wearing the wrong thing, does my hair look bad, am I wearing the right clothes or the right nightgown, is the house clean enough? I am depressed, sad, have loss of motivation and have to hide it, because I'm thinking that will be another reason for him not to want me. I feel betrayed, like I've been cheated on, because he is pleasuring himself while thinking about someone else. This makes me feel ugly, not sexy and unwanted.*

Stephanie (Spouse): *I have lost the playfulness, the enjoyment, the longing, the love, the bonding between a man and a wife.*

Rose (Anorexic): *I continued to experience even worse consequences in my marriage and personal, mental health life.*

Miriam (Spouse): *When we are connecting and becoming close, I let down my guard and I want to become intimate with him. When it turns out that he's not able to go there and he pulls/pushes back, my feelings are even more hurt due to the closeness I had begun to enjoy and value. We are experts in the "dance of intensity" rather than "intimacy."*

4. Keeping it Going

I don't know if you have seen the movie *Planes, Trains and Automobiles* with Steve Martin and John Candy. It's a story of two guys traveling across America trying to arrive at a certain destination. It seems at almost every turn there were terrible things that would happen (consequences). Regardless of any consequence, they were determined to keep going and even when it became extremely ridiculous, they kept their commitment.

This is a great picture of an addict of any kind. They are committed to their addiction. They incur loss after loss, consequence after consequence, but instead of getting sober to what is happening, they get more committed to the addiction and keeping it going. You see, they continue to use their "drug", regardless of the consequences.

I've had intimacy anorexics who have been separated repeatedly, have their children hate them, have a spouse depressed, gained weight and are angry due to the anorexia, and they keep withholding. I've had anorexics starve their spouses sexually until bad things happen. I've seen usage of anorexia after severe consequences, but the anorexic hardens their resolve to withhold. It's quite amazing. In the space provided, circle if that specific anorexic behavior continued to be used even after significant consequences.

	Intimacy Anorexic	Spouse
Busy	Y N	Y N
Blame	Y N	Y N
Withholding Love	Y N	Y N
Withholding Praise	Y N	Y N
Withholding Sex	Y N	Y N
Withholding Spirituality	Y N	Y N
Feelings	Y N	Y N
Criticism	Y N	Y N
Anger/Silence	Y N	Y N
Money	Y N	Y N

Below are some comments from anorexics and spouses of anorexics. These comments can help illustrate efforts an anorexic has had at attempting to stop anorexic behaviors and not being successful.

Rachel (Spouse): *We had a huge fight and I told him that I was done and that we needed to part company. He started to read his Bible like crazy and read other recovery material but his behavior never changed. I confronted him about giving the illusion of change but no tangible change. That was last night, we are not speaking today.*

Todd (Anorexic): *Just a week ago, my wife attempted to initiate sex with me and I turned her down flatly. Later, once I got back on track and realized that I was pulling away from her again, I apologized. She was great about it, but I could see on her face and in her voice the pain that my rejection caused her. I didn't just say no, but I stared a fight with her over it.*

Tanya (Anorexic): *Even though I don't like the distance in my relationships, I still default to withholding as a defense mechanism.*

Titus (Spouse): *Sometimes after we have a bad argument, things will get better for a couple of days and even a week, but then we go back to our old pattern.*

Claire (Spouse): *This has gone on for so long now. I don't care if I won't speak to him, sleep in another room because of the tension in the bedroom, cry, just talk about it, or go for counseling. Nine months can still go by; he doesn't seem to be affected by it, which is not good. He probably thinks, "Well she stayed this long."*

Stephanie (Spouse): *Life as it is now is the consequence of his consistent withholding and control. Our marriage is a charade. It has no fun, no playfulness, no longing, no joy. Not much hope, if any. It is like two strangers in the same existence of a cell.*

Miriam (Spouse): *Most consequences we've tried have to do with him losing an opportunity to engage in a family celebration/event. Sometimes he's so down on himself and others that he doesn't really care and even believes he "deserves" to be cut-off from me and from the family. He kind of enjoys his solitary pity-party and the lack of expectations that come from being alone and not accountable to anyone else.*

5. Do more, Do More

In addiction, there is a place where you get obsessed. This is found in the sex addict who does more and more porn, staying up to 3:00 a.m. several days in a row. The cocaine addict may empty their savings to use more and more, or the debtor who gets another credit card when they can't pay the last three they already have.

Doing more is increasing the usage of the addictive behavior. Doing more is also a characteristic of the intimacy anorexic. The "do more" than before business includes more blaming now than years ago, there is less love, praise or sex which means they have increased usage of withholding. There could be more anger and increasingly intense anger. How about longer periods and more intense silence. Also, there could be less discussion of feelings as they increase usage of withholding feelings. I think you get the idea. In the below categories of withholding behaviors, mark a Yes or No if you, as the intimacy anorexic, or as the spouse have seen an increase of usage of a specific behavior over the course of the marriage.

	Intimacy Anorexic	Spouse
Busy	Y N	Y N
Blame	Y N	Y N

Withholding Love	Y	N		Y	N
Withholding Praise	Y	N		Y	N
Withholding Sex	Y	N		Y	N
Withholding Spirituality	Y	N		Y	N
Feelings	Y	N		Y	N
Criticism	Y	N		Y	N
Anger/Silence	Y	N		Y	N
Money	Y	N		Y	N

Below are some comments from anorexics and spouses of anorexics. These comments can help illustrate efforts an anorexic has had at increasing anorexic behaviors.

Pat (Spouse): *I am not the one who has withheld affection in any form.*

Virginia (Spouse): *My spouse gets "tired" and takes a lot and naps. He "gets sick" to avoid going out on dates. This is his new way of acting in.*

Tanya (Anorexic): *I have found myself withholding more and more over time with my spouse and especially my children. Through recovery I try to be aware of my withholding and give back instead of taking away from it.*

Titus (Spouse): *Yes, it has been the last two to three years that have gotten worse. It has always been an underlying thing, but like I said, the last year or two have been hell.*

Rose (Anorexic): *I was separated from my spouse three times during our 19 year marriage. Because I didn't know how to control him, I had to ask him to leave so I could at least be in control of myself. The first two times he left things got worse. The last time he left things got better after he returned as we both entered recovery. We were very close to divorce. I had no sense of who I was or what I wanted. I was completely lost and so was he. We had to gradually begin to decide to move together and to say in the marriage and work things out. I became more and more emotionally unstable the more I withheld from him.*

6. Takes More

In the field of addiction we have a term we call tolerance. Tolerance is simply when you build up a resistance to the addiction behavior so you have to do more of the behavior to get a result. Tolerance can also mean you don't get as much out of the behaviors as you once did. Either way, tolerance is frustrating to the addict. What once took a beer for the alcoholic to feel better, now takes whiskey and that might not even be satisfying. What a shopaholic used to get out of spending $50 dollars now takes $500 and it still isn't quite scratching the itch. The workaholic who's up to 70 hours a week, now wants to work more. Tolerance is real and it's really frustrating.

For the intimacy anorexic, tolerance can also occur. What worked to create a little distance now takes a lot more of that behavior to create that same distance. Also the distance isn't paying off like it once did. As the anorexic, you could push your spouse away through withholding and it felt good to get that space between you. Now, you get the distance but somehow don't feel as successful. The distance, aloneness, blaming them for everything just doesn't seem to be working for you anymore. You actually feel more remorse about intentionally creating pain for your spouse than you do happiness to get them away from you.

As the spouse, what you would see in the tolerance qualifier is an amping up of a particular behavior to get your further away. The places where they know they can hurt you get pushed more frequently and with more intensity; it's as if you can feel the blatant intentionality to create pain.

As a spouse you might notice that when he or she used to pull away and then came back, there was at least some energy for the relationship. Tolerance would be evident when avoidance wasn't working; therefore, coming back from withholding is with little or no energy for the relationship. In the space provided, circle where you believe that tolerance, in either doing more, or not getting as much out of a withholding behavior, was experienced.

	Intimacy Anorexic		Spouse	
Busy	Y	N	Y	N
Blame	Y	N	Y	N
Withholding Love	Y	N	Y	N
Withholding Praise	Y	N	Y	N

Withholding Sex	Y	N		Y	N
Withholding Spirituality	Y	N		Y	N
Feelings	Y	N		Y	N
Criticism	Y	N		Y	N
Anger/Silence	Y	N		Y	N
Money	Y	N		Y	N

Below are some comments from anorexics and spouses of anorexics. These comments can help illustrate efforts an anorexic has had at attempting tolerance.

Pat (Spouse): *I have seen my husband's behaviors in this area escalate and nothing has changed. He refuses to change, to grow, to work on our relationship.*

Todd (Anorexic): *My anger and blaming my wife for my problems have increased over time.*

Tanya (Anorexic): *I would have to exaggerate the withholding in order to get my husband to notice that I was withholding.*

7. More Time

All addictions take time. Those who gamble increase their time as the addiction grows. Those that use drugs, alcohol, food or sex also utilize more time as the addiction grows. Even those who hoard, or are anorexic with food use more of their time obsessing about what they are not going to eat that day.

The intimacy anorexic is no different. I'll never forget about one female, intimacy anorexic, I counseled in my office. She said, "I've been thinking about not having sex almost all day!" What she was telling me is that her addiction to withholding was now taking up more of her time in her head.

As an anorexic you could experience using more time thinking about withholding. You could also be guilty of spending more time plotting leaving the house, getting your spouse mad, creating more criticism or just thinking of all kinds of ways to blame them for the marriage.

One way you can evaluate a time increase in anorexic behaviors is to evaluate how much time you are now engaged, in outside activities or relationships, than you were earlier in the marriage. A time increase would be true if you are dating less, having sex less, and there is talk about how your addiction to withholding is taking up more of your time as it has been growing in your soul and life as an anorexic.

As a spouse of an anorexic, you could easily see more of the time disappear from the relationship. You may not be aware of the time in their head consumed with this, but if they have become more creative in withholding from you then you can conclude that a good amount of time went into that creativity. In the space provide, circle Y if you are the anorexic or the spouse who has seen an increase of time over the course of the marriage.

	Intimacy Anorexic	Spouse
Busy	Y N	Y N

Blame	Y	N		Y	N
Withholding Love	Y	N		Y	N
Withholding Praise	Y	N		Y	N
Withholding Sex	Y	N		Y	N
Withholding Spirituality	Y	N		Y	N
Feelings	Y	N		Y	N
Criticism	Y	N		Y	N
Anger/Silence	Y	N		Y	N
Money	Y	N		Y	N

Below are some comments from anorexics and spouses of anorexics. These comments can help illustrate efforts an anorexic has had at attempting to increase time spent on their anorexia.

Virginia (Spouse): *My spouse recently took up the guitar to play in a recovery band. It is good to do something positive; however, he has not added in any relationship or family time.*

Holly (Spouse): *My anorexic spouse spends more time exercising now.*

Tanya (Anorexic): *It takes a lot of time and energy to avoid the person you love. I didn't realize how much easier it was to face life honestly until I got into recovery and began acknowledging my feelings and living life upfront.*

Titus (Spouse): *My wife has a hard time saying no to people. I don't know if it is so she can stay busy or if she just doesn't know how to say no.*

Claire (Spouse): *I have moodiness and sadness. I'm on anti-depressants. He's got the problem and I'm the mess taking the meds.*

Rose (Anorexic): *I withdrew; I was moody and sad, and used dissociation to escape.*

8. The Blues

Every addiction has a dark side. Those who use drugs that go up also have the stories of the down. The shopper has the high in the mall but the regret when the credit card bill comes. The sex addict gets exhilaration in their behavior but also the downside of the shame. As the soul increases its dependence on addiction to medicate or deal with life, it is very common to have withdrawals from the drug when it is not available.

For the anorexic, they would feel withdrawals when they can't escape the marriage relationship. This can often happen on vacations, the holidays when you would have more time or even in the evenings when the plans got changed and it's just the two of you. The internal panic that intimacy, connectedness or sex could now occur can cause withdrawal for the intimacy anorexic. He or she can get really moody, and then employ one after another anorexic behaviors to protect from the closeness that could occur. If they feel for any reason that they cannot retreat to a cell phone, book, computer or just go for a walk they can experience withdrawals. By obtaining some distance (the drink for intimacy anorexics) they can calm back down.

If you, as the spouse or as an anorexic have experienced the intimacy anorexic having withdrawals, you would probably have some stories to tell about this. In the space provided is the list of behaviors. Circle the Y next to the signs of withdrawal when the anorexic could not participate in them due to the circumstances.

	Intimacy Anorexic			Spouse	
Busy	Y	N		Y	N
Blame	Y	N		Y	N
Withholding Love	Y	N		Y	N
Withholding Praise	Y	N		Y	N
Withholding Sex	Y	N		Y	N
Withholding Spirituality	Y	N		Y	N
Feelings	Y	N		Y	N
Criticism	Y	N		Y	N
Anger/Silence	Y	N		Y	N
Money	Y	N		Y	N

Below are some comments from anorexics and spouses of anorexics. These comments can help illustrate efforts an anorexic has with withdrawals.

Rachel (Spouse): *Whenever I make a request for him to live in and engage in a real human relationship he will make excuses not to see me, such as today. Please understand that I have learned how to be very explicit and detailed about what I expect.*

Precious (Spouse): *My husband does stay on the Internet and uses his cell phone for Internet. He is extremely moody, cranky, not the sadness type, nothing is good enough or suits him when he gets this way. He also has a "charming" side that seeks to take attention away from anything he does. But it is all "surface" and there is nothing deep emotionally.*

Todd (Anorexic): *I will use the Internet or especially the TV as my primary means to escape.*

Virginia (Spouse): *My spouse frequently has a "tummy ache" or gets tired or dizzy. The few times we were to go on a date he got sick. If I share my observations or hurt feelings my spouse will start a coughing fit so bad he usually throws up. No doctor has found anything wrong with him except seasonal allergies.*

Holly (Spouse): *My anorexic spouse is withdrawn, moody and sad most of the time.*

Titus (Spouse): *My wife can almost never have a conversation with me unless she is playing games on her cell phone. She says it's too difficult to talk unless she is distracted.*

Monique (Spouse): *My husband has used his computer and the claim that he is working to avoid all kinds of things. He says he is working but is on numerous non-work websites; instead, he stays up till ungodly hours on Facebook and news sites and never seems to have the time to spend with his children or to help around the house. Yes, he also has an Internet addiction. And when challenged, he is quite stoic in his claim that he is working and cannot leave the office "right now."*

9. Increasing Other Activities:

In most addictions, this last symptom of an addiction process is stated in the other direction. The addict decreases the other recreation, social or vocation activities. The idea here is as the addiction grows the addict recoils from their other activities and events to spend more quality time with their addiction regardless of how the addiction is maintained.

For the intimacy anorexic, it is just the opposite. To see them "drink" is to actively withhold from their spouse. So they drink when they are further apart from their spouse or set up scenarios where intimacy is more difficult to accomplish (extended travel, increased responsibilities).

So for the anorexic, there is an increase in recreational and social events outside of the relationship, job time, job responsibilities or volunteering. The increases in these activities decrease the risk of the possibility of intimacy with the spouse. The other thing I have noticed with intimacy anorexics with this symptom, is firstly, there is a growing entitlement to these commitments. One anorexic guy was so entitled to play two rounds of golf every Saturday leaving no time for the marriage or children on the weekend. This entitlement grew over the years with his anorexia.

Secondly, I see money, energy, creativity, rationalizing and defending the time increases in these areas. Protecting, increases time in these events and other relationships grow over time. I learned something important over my twenty plus years of counseling and it's simple...what a person protects is what they love. The spouse feels when the intimacy anorexic protects the time increase in other areas over their marriage.

The anorexic will use the withholding behaviors to try to control the spouse into agreeing to these outside arrangements. Let's just take a moment and see if the anorexic is increasing time in these areas within the marriage.

	Intimacy Anorexic		Spouse	
Busy	Y	N	Y	N
Blame	Y	N	Y	N
Withholding Love	Y	N	Y	N
Withholding Praise	Y	N	Y	N
Withholding Sex	Y	N	Y	N
Withholding Spirituality	Y	N	Y	N

	Intimacy Anorexic		Spouse	
Feelings	Y	N	Y	N
Criticism	Y	N	Y	N
Anger/Silence	Y	N	Y	N
Money	Y	N	Y	N

Now let's look to see if you have seen an increase of the withholding behaviors. Circle yes or no if you see these behaviors used to manipulate increased in activities or extended time.

	Intimacy Anorexic		Spouse	
Busy	Y	N	Y	N
Blame	Y	N	Y	N
Withholding Love	Y	N	Y	N
Withholding Praise	Y	N	Y	N
Withholding Sex	Y	N	Y	N
Withholding Spirituality	Y	N	Y	N
Feelings	Y	N	Y	N
Criticism	Y	N	Y	N
Anger/Silence	Y	N	Y	N
Money	Y	N	Y	N

Below are some comments from anorexics and spouses of anorexics. These comments can help illustrate efforts an anorexic has had at attempting to increase outside activities.

Rachel (Spouse): *There are so many. We were sexual three or more years ago and he informed me last night that he was thinking about other women and he felt badly when he would look in my eyes. He decided that he couldn't anymore, because he was scared the images would come back. This is probably the most truthful thing he has ever said. You can imagine the hurt and betrayal I felt. Especially, because, I asked these questions specifically in the past and he denied them. I came unglued and he stomped out and is still not talking to me and probably will continue for a while.*

Todd (Anorexic): *I can't say that I do this because I hate to leave the house where I might have to deal with others. I'd rather be at home where I can predict the behaviors of my family members rather than be around others that I don't know as well and can't predict.*

Virginia (Spouse): *My spouse goes to two men's groups a week. He has taken up the guitar. He does not do anything special for our relationship. We have been to three counselors; he agreed to follow the program and then doesn't. My spouse then blames me.*

Holly (Spouse): *My anorexic spouse keeps his physical distance to avoid intimacy.*

Tanya (Anorexic): *I would overcommit myself to volunteer work. These weren't things that I enjoyed. I just did them to look good in the community and fill my time. As I write this,*

I realize that intimacy was what I was craving. I don't think I was busy to avoid intimacy, but to fill my time because of my husband's rejection of me.

Titus (Spouse): *My wife will go away overnight once in a while to see our grandson, but it is not enough. She wants to go at least once a week to see our grandson and help out our kids, but sometimes in the past this turned into a couple of days.*

Monique (Spouse): *My husband doesn't miss a meeting (especially networking-type meetings), and says he has more important things to do than to do the homework his counselor assigned to him. He loves to be on committees.*

Nancy (Spouse): *He stays busy with sports, kids, sports, palm pilot, Yahtzee, sports, TV, playing cards, internet porn, sports, and kids.*

Now put all your answers in one location. For each area place a general yes or no for the anorexic and one from the spouse. If they are significantly different I would lean toward the spouse's answers unless they are also an intimacy anorexic.

	Intimacy Anorexic	Spouse
Busy	Y N	Y N
Blame	Y N	Y N
Withholding Love	Y N	Y N
Withholding Praise	Y N	Y N

Withholding Sex	Y	N	Y N
Withholding Spirituality	Y	N	Y N
Feelings	Y	N	Y N
Criticism	Y	N	Y N
Anger/Silence	Y	N	Y N
Money	Y	N	Y N

Total Yes _____   Total No _____

Remember the process you just went through is the same type of screening an addict of any kind would go through to determine if this behavior is an addiction. So if you are the intimacy anorexic don't get mad at your spouse, me or the universe, if your score is not what you like. If you're the spouse of an intimacy anorexic, congratulations, you most likely wrote a huge check to get your marriage to this point of clarity.

If there are three or more yes answers you could easily say, "Hi, my name is _____, and I am an intimacy anorexic." That means you are reading the right book and you and your marriage can recover from this secret addiction that has been destroying your marriage.

6

Addiction Continuum

Addictions often run in continuums. You can have an extreme anorexic on one or either end of the continuum or have both extremes in the same person. Let me give you some examples of what I am talking about before I apply this to the intimacy anorexic addiction process.

Let's talk about food since that is something we are all very familiar with. On the one side of the continuum we have the overeater. This person uses food to medicate to the point where their body suffers enormously. Then, on the other side of that same continuum of food, there is the food anorexic. They are often addicted to not eating to the point of severe damage to their body.

Another example of an addiction continuum is dealing with money. On one side of this continuum, we have the spender/debtor. This person medicates themselves by spending. They shop when they feel pain or boredom even if they don't have the money and wind up hurting themselves and their family financially. On the other side of that continuum is the money anorexic saver/hoarder type. This person could be worth millions but can't give money away or celebrate with money at all. I think you can see where I am going with this as we talk about intimacy anorexia.

On the intimacy anorexia continuum we also have two polar opposites. Here we are going to take the time to look at both sides of the continuum as well as the middle, which is the healthy place, so we know where we are going.

Often, when I am explaining this to my phone clients I ask them to draw something to help them visualize this. I can tell them to draw two circles, one on each side of the paper and a square in the middle. I use the example of a car with two headlights and a grill in the middle.

Remember, in our field for years we called intimacy anorexia, sexual anorexia and the intimacy anorexia would be on the left side of the square and the sexual addiction would be on the right side.

Anorexia Side: Here are some core ideas on intimacy anorexia. The first thing that is obvious on the intimacy anorexia side of this continuum is that because of the addiction to withholding and the emotional immaturity of the intimacy anorexic, there is a lack of intimacy in the marriage. This is like saying the food anorexic is skinny. The objective of anorexia creates this devastation for both people in the marriage. Unlike the food anorexic whose only body that is suffering is their own, the intimacy anorexic's addiction is much crueler, it starves itself and starves its spouse intentionally making both people suffer.

Often it is the spouse who suffers more and may even be made to look like the problem due to the intimacy anorexic's behavior.

This leads me to the second big idea of intimacy anorexia. This will be really hard to swallow for the intimacy anorexic because of the desire to be in the good box. However, when it comes to the spouse, the reality of other people (their spouse) has little or no value to them.

Immediately, the intimacy anorexic wants to rise up and say that's not true; I love my spouse. I say, I believe you have feelings for your spouse and at times feel love, but let's talk about your pet for a moment. If you treated your pet for years by withholding its food except enough to barely survive, blamed it for the problems in your life, yelled at it, criticized it, didn't celebrate it, only touched it if it cried loud enough to wake the neighbors, that's not really what I would call love. "I guess not Doc," is usually a response. The anorexic does have a love for the spouse but is mostly expressed in an emotionally limited way as any addict might. This would be like having a rich parent who is money anorexic and every birthday you get a dollar in your birthday card. They care, but they're not going to spend beyond what is safe for them.

Thirdly, the focus of anorexia is avoidance. They are addicted to withholding and not giving of themselves. They strategize to stay disconnected. Now, often they are not aware of this until it's pointed out to them by someone on the outside. However, it is intentional behavior creating or maintaining distance. So, when an intimacy anorexic is engaged in avoidant or maintaining avoidance, they are in the middle of drinking in their addiction, often oblivious to the pain they are causing themselves or their spouse.

Lastly, the skills in their addiction are any and all manipulations that create distance. Later I will discuss more of these strategies, but for now I want to express that they are skills and they are refined skills over time as they weaken their spouses or discover new weaknesses in the spouses.

Most addicts refine their skills over time. The food addict can tell you the best ice cream, donut shop or even the best steakhouse in town. The spendaholic can tell you the best stores and when these stores have their best sales for anything you could want, so you can buy more for less (that's heaven for the spender).

So, over time, the intimacy anorexic gets better at additional methods for intentionally creating pain for the spouse to create distance. If silence drives them crazy, they apply more. If anger works, it would become more intense, or more often. If it is shaming that causes a lack of sexual desire to be creative and random or to not want to be sexual then there would be more of this. Once you dig a little deeper into any addiction, it is insidious; the intimacy anorexia is no different in that respect. It gets quite dark as you go further into this disease.

Intimacy Anorexia

- Little to no intimacy
- Spouse has little value
- Avoidance is focus
- Skills increase to avoid

Addiction Side: The addiction side on this same continuum is the sexual addiction. Remember, many, if not most, men with intimacy anorexia have an active sexual addiction. Let me take a moment to discuss this before I give you the big ideas on this side of the continuum.

The majority of intimacy anorexics that are sex addicts, male or female are primarily addicted to withholding with a secondary addiction to sex. You see their core addiction is withholding but they still want sex, not intimacy or making love, but sex. This type of sex is disconnected from relationships.

For the anorexic, sex with a fantasy world of porn is perfect. This is the ultimate sex since it is without relationship. They give nothing and receive their fix of sex and usually some adoration. The men that are anorexic, if they use others for sex, will often utilize prostitutes (sex without intimacy or commitment). You see, they want to be sexual but not intimate.

Now let's walk though the big ideas on the sex addiction side. Firstly, like on the anorexia side, there is no intimacy. For the fantasy, porn, and masturbation sex addict, there can't be intimacy. The images or fantasies are unable to be intimate. The sex addict creates whatever he or she wants the other world to be and connects to the ideas of that world, not to the person. Remember also that addiction dwarfs you emotionally, so even if it's another person, rarely is the addict intimate with them. This brings me to my second point.

On this side of the continuum, people also have little to no value (those they act out with). The stripper, prostitute or even the ongoing partner who is willing to have sex without intimacy or commitment means little to nothing to the sex addict. Hundreds of addicts, even if they are having sex for years with someone, when asked if they loved the other person they will say, "No, it's just sex." They see the other person as an object and a means to an end, sex.

Thirdly, the focus for the sex addict is self pleasure. On this side of the continuum, the focus of the addict is self pleasure e.g., the getting off, getting the chemical high from sex, and the rush of secrecy. They are chasing an ever illusive high in sexually acting out. They create different scenarios for acting out just like the intimacy anorexic creates scenarios to avoid.

Lastly, the skill in the sex addiction side is manipulation for pleasure. They have to manipulate their time to act out with self or others. They have to create stories and lies to hide their addiction behaviors. For some, they have to manipulate money to make their addiction happen. Regardless of what they have to do, they are committed to do whatever they have to in order to get their sexual pleasure.

Sexual Addiction

- No intimacy
- People they act out with have no value
- Focused on self pleasure
- Skill is to manipulate for pleasure

Intimacy/Sexual Health: In the middle of this continuum is intimacy and sexuality that is healthy. I want to share this with you, so you have an idea of the goal in recovery. I will say that you will only get there if the intimacy anorexic does their work and the spouse heals from the past consequences. If both are intimacy anorexics then this goal is reached only if both do active recovery. If the intimacy anorexic is also a sex addict, he or she must be in recovery, for both withholding and sex, to reach to the center of the continuum. In my experiences from counseling, when I have seen some of these combinations fail to get to the middle of the continuum, it is because one partner won't do the hard work that recovery demands. On a good note, I have regularly seen each combination become successful as both in the marriage work their recovery and go through the healing process. To quote a cliché, they "lived happily ever after."

In this part of the continuum, intimacy is present and expressed regularly. This couple can and does consistently connect emotionally, spiritually and sexually. They either innately have the tools and the discipline of intimacy, or they learned them along the way, and applied them consistently to get results. They connect on all three levels regularly.

Secondly, in the healthy part of this continuum, people have value. A soul, including and especially the spouse, has great value. Both can hear each other but not necessarily agree. Respect for each other is present. People are not objects; they are souls and are priceless in this quadrant of the continuum.

Thirdly, the focus of this continuum is to mutually nurture and bring pleasure to each other. They know how the other person receives love and gives that to them. They know the other person sexually and giving to them is a natural part of the process. There is no strain to give or receive love. Is it a utopia? No, they're still human. But being human, flawed and loved is acceptable. They can be honest, ask for forgiveness, move on and both give this grace to each other in the marriage.

Lastly, the skills here are that of emotional intimacy (sharing feelings), spiritual connection, sexual consistency and the skill of negotiating through the issues of life. This isn't a one up, one down place, but a place where souls are different but equal, flawed and loved and encouraged to grow. This is a place of health where each person takes full responsibility for themselves and responsibility without dread to give to the other person. In this place, love, honor and cherish is taken responsibly till death do they part.

Health

- Intimacy expressed
- People (especially spouse) have value
- Focus of nurturing and pleasuring each other
- Skills are for intimacy and negotiation

Now, let's put these three parts of the continuum side by side again for a moment. Look at the chart and compare.

Intimacy Anorexia

- Spouse has little value
- Avoidance is focus
- Skills increase to avoid pleasure

Sexual Addiction

- Little to no intimacy
- No intimacy
- People that act out with have no value

- Focused on self pleasure
- Skill is to manipulate for pleasure

Health

- Intimacy expressed
- People (especially spouse) have value
- Focus of nurturing and pleasuring each other
- Skills are for intimacy and negotiation

In these charts, it is striking how similar the addiction patterns are. They both don't have intimacy as a result of their addiction. They both don't value people e.g., the addict, those they use to act out with, the intimacy anorexic, and the person they are married to. They both have clear objectives-avoidance for the intimacy anorexic and pleasure for the addict. They both have a set of skills to achieve their objectives. These are similar indeed and both are active addiction processes.

I find it helpful for clients to see both addiction processes (sexual addiction and the withholding addiction). For those that have both addiction processes, they interrelate. They will act in on the spouse and act out with the fantasy world or others. Each addiction reinforces the other and that's why both need to be in remission for healing to occur.

Every marriage deserves to aim toward the middle. It will take work for you both to get and stay there. I can tell you professionally that for almost two decades I have seen many happy endings. My hope, as you continue to read and do the work, is that you will also find your own *happily ever after*.

Anorexic Strategies

Earlier we discussed the characteristics of intimacy anorexia. Those characteristics continue steadily over the course of the marriage. In this chapter I'll share with you two major strategies that many intimacy anorexics utilize to create distance. After defining each strategy I'll explain how to identify an anorexic strategy that the intimacy anorexic might be using.

Starve the Dog

As you may know, when you live with an addiction in your marriage it can significantly impact the spouse. As simple as that principle is, it is often overlooked by most anorexics. If I said that someone you knew was an alcohol, drug or sex addict, would you agree that this addiction impacted the spouse of the addict? Most people would say "of course!"

Remember, the intimacy anorexic wants to live in the good box. They are not so good at seeing the affects of intentionally withholding from their spouse. That plays into their spouse's responses and how the intimacy anorexic sets it up to be that way.

When I counsel a couple with one or both of them being intimacy anorexic, I have a story I tell them so they will understand this point. I call the story, "starve the dog." Starving the dog is a major intimacy anorexic strategy that I have seen in nearly all marriages where one or both have intimacy anorexia.

Here is the story. When I was younger, I learned a lot about dogs. Sometimes, it seemed that we had more dogs than people in our family. I love dogs, and I think dogs are great (sorry, I'm allergic to cats). It is fairly simple if you want to raise a nice dog within a family. You feed the puppy consistently, you pet, play and talk to the dog and the dog will make a nice pet for almost any family.

However, not every family or business wants a nice dog. Some want a mean dog to protect a property. So if you want a mean dog you take a perfectly good and nice puppy and you starve the dog. I don't mean you don't feed it. Maybe you feed it irregularly, you never talk to the dog and you don't touch it. That dog will become a mean dog. Regardless of how nice the dog was as a puppy, over time because its needs were not being met, this intentional deprivation has a predictable outcome of altering the dog. The dog becomes mean, unapproachable and altered. The on-looker of this dog thinks, "Wow, what a mean dog." The perceptive onlooker might think, "Wow, a cruel and intentionally mean owner has created that dog."

Intimacy anorexia intentionally puts their spouse in deprivation for years or decades. They ignore the emotional, spiritual and/or the three dimensional sexual needs of their spouse. They intentionally withhold love, praise, and sex, and then blame their spouse and use anger or silence to push them away. This intentional pain given to the spouse significantly impacts them over time and alters their spouse over time.

Because of this depravation, the spouse acts angry, depressed, critical, gains weight, and has lower self esteem. The anorexic then focuses on their spouse's reactions to the withholding and often seeks pity because of the person they live with, thus playing the victim instead of owning that they are the perpetrator of the pain causing this altered spouse.

If you lived with this insanity or you are creating this insanity you know exactly what I mean. I had one female anorexic client who hasn't had sex with her husband for eight months and couldn't understand why he was so angry. Talk about denial!

If you are in a marriage where one or both of you are intimacy anorexic, then you have lived through this scenario countless times. I hope this helps you make sense of this intentional strategy, where the anorexic makes the spouse look crazy. If you both have intimacy anorexia then the game is really interesting as you both sabotage each other with "starve the dog." Here are some comments from anorexics and spouses regarding this strategy.

Helen (Spouse): *My ex-husband would stay in his car, across the street from home, waiting until I left home. Then he'd* come in the house, watch TV, shower, eat, and sleep. When I caught him doing this he blamed me for spying on him and not giving him freedom to come and go as he pleases.

Todd (Anorexic): *My wife suggested that we spend some time together one evening. I agreed. But during the day, I got tired at work and am not feeling great in the evening. My wife asked again if we were going to spend some time together and I got angry at her that she is not recognizing that I don't feel good.*

Virginia (Spouse): *Recently, I shared how I was noticing we haven't had any couple time lately, although my spouse had time to go to two men's meetings a week. He instantly blamed me and stated we had "five minutes" together yesterday. Then he started yelling and got into an argument with me. I shut the bedroom door so the kids would not hear us and he threw a book at the wall so hard it dented the drywall. He blamed all of this on me. He was going to Bible study and it was the Bible he threw at the wall. It has taken him four weeks to repair the wall because he was so busy.*

Holly (Spouse): *No hugs, holding hands, or kisses for days, and when I confronted him, he said that I was being aloof to him so he did not feel wanted.*

Titus (Spouse): *If I start to complain about not having sex for several weeks she will tell me that it is because I am complaining about it and that makes her not want to have sex and that it is not fair for me to put pressure on her since I am aware of how she feels about sex. She will suggest that there is a problem with me for my wanting sex so often even through it has been a couple of weeks since we made love.*

Sam (Anorexic): *I would not pursue her by hand holding or cuddling and yet get mad at her when I am denied sex.*

Monique (Spouse): *Oh my, does this ever sound familiar! This was the classic story with us prior to our separation. My husband doesn't have enough time to spend with me, so my emotional needs don't get met. He "needs to get this job completed" before coming to bed, so I go to bed without him, and then he complains that we don't have sex often enough. When he does come to me for sex, I am not feeling "in the mood" because I need his emotional closeness, but as soon as I suggest that we talk first or do something else together he becomes critical and says that I am not meeting his needs. Then he throws in the accusation that if I don't meet his sexual needs, he will cave into self behaviors and/ or turn to porn. How he thinks that saying something like that is a turn-on is a mystery to me! I end up backing away, and then get blamed more for not meeting his needs.*

Claire (Spouse): *In my case, after months of my husband withholding sex, I'm actually hurt but wind up acting mean because I'm so upset and then he says, "When you act like this, why would I want to have sex?" Maybe this sounds crazy, but sometimes I catch myself almost acting like that on purpose thinking what I did caused it, and not because he really doesn't want me.*

Abby (Anorexic): *When we are in bed and I roll over, he takes it as rejection or disinterest. I hear sighs and disappointment. There is no action on either one of our parts, no dialog, no touch, no questions, just starvation. I recoil, go inside myself, turn to silence, non verbals, and basically give up. Then I am the prude. I don't ever want to do it. But really, it is almost a relief for both of us.*

Read Their Mind

A second and very common strategy for intimacy anorexia is to intentionally create distance and pain for their spouse by what I call "read their mind." Let me tell you how this strategy plays out so you can be informed as you will mostly likely encounter this strategy, frequently, as a spouse of an anorexic.

Remember that the intimacy anorexic wants to live in a reality where they are always good. To do that, the spouse of the intimacy anorexic has to be the bad person according to intimacy anorexic's reality. Let's suppose that you have a reasonably descent spouse (which by the way is relatively common). The spouse is being descent and even kind and thoughtful, thinking they are feeling close and that there is the possibility that intimacy or even sex could occur. Remember that intimacy (emotionally, spiritually or sexually) is what the intimacy anorexic is trying to avoid. What does an anorexic do when intimacy is happening spontaneously? The anorexic reads their spouse's mind.

That's right, most intimacy anorexics have secret superhero powers to read minds. Interestingly enough, this super power only works with their spouse and it can only read negative thoughts or intentions, even if they are not there in reality. I call this the "intimacy anorexia fantasy."

They create only the worst fantasies about their spouse such as, "They are only being nice because they want sex." "They are buttering me up for money or to manipulate me." "This is a scam." "Don't trust them; you know they're going to hurt you." "This is really for them to feel good about themselves; they don't care about me." The negative list goes on for eternity. Now, again, there is no reality to this thinking.

The intimacy anorexic needs to be rescued from potential intimacy. The "I can read your mind" strategy, comes to the rescue. Now, because they now believe their spouse is bad, negative, critical or up to something (and this is important) they can justify withholding and punishing them or pushing them away by implementing any intimacy anorexia characteristic.

This is important because now they can put their spouse intentionally in pain and yet be completely justified (good person) even though what they are doing is intentionally creating pain for the spouse. The "read your mind" strategy is as crazy making as it gets for the spouse. The intimacy anorexic creates a negative reality that's not true, becomes judge, jury and executioner of their spouse's sins. Whatever they deem just, whammo, you are more distant than you were before.

If you have done this or lived through this repeatedly, I do understand. Addiction is not fun for anyone. This intimacy anorexic strategy is usually present with intimacy anorexia. Here are some comments from anorexics and spouses regarding the "read their mind" strategy.

Pat (Spouse): *He says things I did not say, tries to put words into my mouth that I did not say, accuses me of things I did not do nor intended to do.*

Todd (Anorexic): *If my wife expresses any kind of feeling bad or tired that day, when I first come home from work, I* interpret that as her not wanting to be around me. I then disappear for the rest of the evening with TV or the Internet.

Virginia (Spouse): *My spouse usually assumes without asking me. My spouse is a teacher and would not get a summer job last year because he thought I would "divorce him and take him for all his money." He was very mad and angry at me all summer and would not help out at home.*

Titus (Spouse): *Sometimes, when we are in a discussion, I will say something that she will misunderstand. Once I am aware that she misunderstood my meaning, I will try to explain what I actually meant, but she will say to me, "That's not what you said," and hold onto the negative meaning even though I am desperately trying to explain what I was actually trying to say. She will hold me to my words even when they are known to be misunderstood. She chooses to hold onto the negative meaning that she interpreted. Many times, I will say something that is not meant as an attack, just a fact like, "Honey, I am out of white clothes" or "We are out of milk" and she will react in anger with much outrage about how she just did the laundry and how could I be out. She responds to me like I was trying to say something negative about her, when in fact, I was just stating a fact that I wanted her to be aware of.*

Stephanie (Spouse): *He laughs with his colleagues and clients on the phone. He TALKS with them. He is communicative. He makes conversation. I get to hear this all the time because he works from home. I have brought up on several occasions how he is, especially when he does all this with the females. He says it is just business. Funny thing is, this is just a marriage. He can't be bothered with the same exercise of effort? He stopped trying not long after we* married. From what I understand, he was this way with his previous wife and with his family. So I can't take it personally. But, I can admit that it is not how I wish to spend the rest of MY life.

Tanya (Anorexic): My husband would ignore me, not have sex with me, and leave me to myself. After about six months, I would confront him very aggressively. He could always turn the tables and say that I had been too busy for him, or that I was spending so much time with the children, I didn't have time for him.

Miriam (Spouse): Recently, I called him after an argument to try to reconnect. He was busy, and said he'd call right back, but didn't. After not hearing from him, I unsuccessfully tried to call him and got no answer. Later in the day, I called and even though he admitted to having left his phone in the car where he couldn't hear it ring, he accused me of "blowing him off." He couldn't even acknowledge that the "facts" didn't support this, but he was still REALLY angry about it.

Rose (Anorexic): I would read the mind of my spouse and know he had negative intentions and hated me, and so withdrew even more and would be unavailable for him even more.

How to Know

In this section I will help you identify the many anorexic strategies. Each couple presents a set of unique intimacy anorexic strategies that work to intentionally create distance and pain for their particular spouse. Intimacy anorexia is adaptive and if the anorexic remarries they adapt to create different strategies for the next spouse to keep them away and the strategies for the second spouse are slightly different from the strategies used for their first spouse.

Here, I'll outline three clear principles for you to be able to identify an intimacy anorexic strategy, whether you are the spouse or the intimacy anorexic. As you read through this section, you might have flashes of identifying intimacy anorexic strategies that are or have been active in your marriage. If this occurs, I highly recommend that you write them down and then run them through the grid I am going to present. If the behavior passes all three tests, it probably is an intentional strategy to create distance in the relationship and pain for the spouse.

Exclusive to You

If you identify a behavior that seems to be exclusive to you, this would be your first warning. Sometimes it might be applied to your children. Let's suppose you are the only person your souse is late for, everywhere and everyone else, they are on time or early—this is a strategy to keep you angry, rejected and distant and to make you look crazy when you get upset.

Now, if they are late for everybody all the time or they are A.D.D., then it's global, not specific to you, and could be a personality flaw. Another element to look at, regarding a strategy, is if it's an area that they know causes you great pain.

Let's say the anorexic knows something shameful or something that you did that was not a good idea, and they know it shuts you down and is painful to you and this is what they bring up privately or publicly to create pain and distance. You have never seen them do this to anyone else but you. You just discovered an intentional intimacy anorexia strategy.

So, if it's exclusively to you and/or knowingly creates pain for you as the spouse, you have taken the first step in identifying an intimacy anorexia strategy. Here are some comments from anorexics and spouses regarding "exclusive to you."

Rachel (Spouse): *He calls his friends and acquaintances and tells them all about what is happening with him. I find things out as a result of the conversations.*

Pat (Spouse): *I see my spouse as charming and so easy to get along with EVERYONE else but me. I am the dog he kicks.*

Helen (Spouse): *I found my ex-husband making friends with waitresses all over town in restaurants, coffee shops, and truck stops, spending hours talking with them, but he was telling me he had to leave home to go to work.*

Pam (Spouse): *He is always doing things for others, taking them places, giving them compliments, but I never get these things.*

Todd (Anorexic): *I am considered to be a wonderful Cub Scout Cubmaster. I am really energetic about it and the boys love being there and talking to me about what is going on in their lives. I rarely have the same energy and engagement with my own wife.*

Virginia (Spouse): *Everybody thinks my spouse is a saint because he is a music teacher. What they don't know is that he will not even help his own children with their music lessons* at home. My spouse will do anything they ask of him at his work, but does not listen or hear me when we have a need. An example of this is when we were to attend a marriage conference at a beautiful resort. My spouse came home one hour late, because he was doing "work", when we could have been having fun at the resort. Another example of this is my spouse "invited" me on a birthday overnighter. He told me to be ready at 2:00 p.m. He showed up at home at 4:00 p.m. because he was out doing other errands. Then he didn't understand why I was "hurt." He acts like he is the one who got hurt.

Holly (Spouse): He will do anything for his child and puts his child first, before me, on all levels.

Titus (Spouse): My wife will pour out all kinds of affection on our grandson and kids, kisses, hugs but when I bring up in counseling that I want physical affection from her, like a kiss when I come home or a hug, she says that I am asking too much of her. Many times when I go to give her a kiss she will turn her head at the last second and give me her cheek. This happens all the time and is very disheartening.

Sam (Anorexic): All of our friends thought I was the best and this fed my need for approval.

Tanya (Anorexic): My husband doesn't find himself very attractive so he imagines that I see him the same way. He believes that if I don't have sex with him for a certain length of time (even if he is sabotaging sexual encounters) that I find him disgusting and ugly.

Nancy (Spouse): I waited more than six months for him to fix my brakes, but the neighbor asked him to fix hers and he *was on it in thirty minutes. I had to pay to have mine done and they cost twice as much.*

Rose (Anorexic): *I was wonderful to others. Withholding from my spouse included spending lots of time with my relatives and girlfriends, but avoiding spending any time with my husband.*

Effective

The next step is for you, as the anorexic or the spouse, to determine if this particular behavior is an amazing strategy and effective in creating distance. Effective is crucial for a behavior to be an intimacy anorexic behavior strategy.

If, at the end of a behavior, you are further apart or much further apart you have most likely been slimed by the addiction to withholding. As a spouse you may feel as if you don't know what just happened, or how you got there since you were getting along so well. This feeling you have is a successful intimacy anorexic strategy.

I have had telephone sessions with couples that are both anorexic and they are both relapsing, blaming, angry and critical. After about ten minutes of sliming me with thieir active addiction, reality hits and I say, "Congratulations."

That immediately stops the conversation because they were both hoping I would take their side and condemn the other one responsible for this dysfunction. I then say, "Congratulations, you both want to be distant and you both were successful at creating this."

For an intimacy anorexia behavior to be effective, it has to create distance. So if you have a behavior that, firstly, is exclusively to you and, secondly, is effective at creating distance, then you are now ready to take this behavior to the final analysis to see if it qualifies for an intentional intimacy anorexia strategy. If you're the anorexic and you're still having difficulty with the word intentional, that's okay. As you get sober you will see that your frustration and anger about this is part of your addiction to withholding.

Repeated

If the behavior you are questioning is repeated and getting predictable results, you have an intentional intimacy anorexia strategy. Either one of you could see this pattern. The intimacy anorexic does X behavior and gets Y (distance) as a result almost every time they do X behavior.

This is known as cause and effect. If I do X (get angry at you, blame you) I can almost guarantee distance, then the intimacy anorexic has found a successful tool to intentionally create distance. If you're the spouse, you might think, "Why would someone do this?" It's insane.

Insane it is, like any addiction behavior. In the Twelve Steps of recovery, addicts of any kind are restored to sanity as they get sober. As the intimacy anorexic gets sober they too will eventually say, "What was I thinking?" This happens to all addicts as they get sober. Until then they'll justify, drink till 3:00 a.m., spend money they don't have, and break the law to act out in their addiction.

The intimacy anorexic will have all kinds of reasons to justify their intimacy anorexic behavior. Most of it will have to do with blaming the spouse or being the victim, so be prepared for that if you are the spouse. I hope this discussion on anorexic strategies has been helpful. I use the acronym EER to make it simple to remember.

E = Exclusive (to you)
E = Effective (to create distance)
R = Repeated

If you see EER in your own behavior as the anorexic, write them down. This will be important to intentionally dismantle in your sobriety. If you're a spouse, you can be aware of them and not give the intended result as this frustrates the desired result of the anorexic momentarily.

There is hope as the intimacy anorexic looks at these strategies and accepts full responsibility for the intention and desired effect of these behaviors. When you see the taking on of responsibility, then you are in the middle of the miracle of recovery. My hope is that as you both read on, your marriage can be one of those miracles I see, all the time, in my office in Colorado Springs.

Intimacy Anorexia: The Book

8

The Friends of Anorexia

Now I want to take you on a real adventure inside the intimacy anorexia world. In this world of intimacy anorexia there are friends to meet. Each friend plays a contributing role to keeping the intimacy anorexia structure intact. These friends play a supportive role to the intimacy anorexic. This would be much like an alcoholic having drinking buddies or the shopaholic having shopping buddies. Addicts, like most people, like to have support for their activities. Unlike other addictions where the addict's "buddies" are real people, the intimacy anorexic's buddies are quite different.

The intimacy anorexic's buddies are internal buddies. These buddies are lodged deep in the intimacy anorexic's heart. For most intimacy anorexics, they are unaware of these buddies and the significant role they play in their lives, until they are pointed out.

As the spouse, you probably have seen these buddies repeatedly; you just didn't know their names. As a spouse, the identification of these buddies will help you to identify if the anorexic has been "drinking" with these buddies to gain support to justify withholding from you.

As the anorexic identifies these buddies, it might be painful, as it plays to the darker side of themselves. That side is not the good boy or girl so try to stay open minded and weigh if this or that buddy is a part of you or your anorexic's life. Not all intimacy anorexics have each buddy, but most anorexic's have more than they think. At the end of the chapter, I will give you a place for each of you to check off which buddies you see that are being supportive of the intimacy anorexic.

Victim

This is probably the most common friend of the anorexic. I have seen this buddy over and over during the many years counseling intimacy anorexics. The victim tells the anorexic how they are the victim of their spouse. The victim turns almost any conflict or circumstance and spins it (amazingly quickly) on how they are the victim. This victim is almost a reflexive response so the speed of this buddy is lightening fast. I have actually seen the anorexic's spouse walk away thinking they really were the problem and accepted the blame repeatedly.

As a spouse, if you see the victim, understand that this is an emotional state, not a rational state. You cannot reason with the victim, you must stay in your reality to survive. As the intimacy anorexic, if you feel the victim emerging, you will usually have to slow down, call a support person and run your thoughts by them before you submit to the victim. This "buddy" will push your spouse away and you might begin acting in. Let me explain how this works from the anorexic's perspective.

The intimacy anorexic intentionally starves the spouse. The spouse is legitimately angry or critical of this neglect and pain, but the victim says, "you're being abused by your spouse; he or she disrespects you, and doesn't appreciate you." You see, now the anorexic who is actually the perpetrator gets to believe and behave as the victim. In *Intimacy Anorexia: The Workbook,* I have intimacy anorexic's write a thank you and goodbye letter to this buddy, the victim. Below are some comments from anorexics and their spouses about the victim.

Holly (Spouse): *As the anorexic, my husband blames me and plays the victim of neglect.*

Ted (Anorexic): *Mainly this is played out inside my head. I will tell myself that I am not understood, no one cares about me.*

Claire (Spouse): *Everything is about how it affects my husband. He's always the victim and it's always about him. I have to say, "Wait a minute; we are talking about me right now, not you."*

Abby (Anorexic): *He works so hard and deserves to zone out on the computer or TV all night. He leave me alone mentality.*

Miriam (Spouse): *He says, "'No one has ever understood me', 'Everyone expects too much of me', 'I didn't really tell a lie; I just didn't tell the truth' 'Why are you so upset?'"*

Fantasy Person

This is a real trouble-making friend of the intimacy anorexic. This is the fantasy where almost any person other than the spouse will love, appreciate, and unconditionally accept them more than their spouse, while not asking for sex or intimacy. For the most part, this is a fantasy. Sometimes it takes the role of pornography or romantic novel characters.

There is a place for some anorexics where they will recruit real people. They will be nice to them, flirt with them, and have conversations that might be questionable but wont touch or kiss them. This is what I call emotional pornography.

The intimacy anorexic scans the person's imagined features then uses them to romanticize or sexualize what life would be like with them. This drives the spouse crazy because they can sense this energy between them. The intimacy anorexic will deny this because "they are good and haven't done anything wrong."

The fantasy person plays two roles of support for the addiction to withholding process. Firstly, it's the role of criticizing the spouse to justify ill treatment of them through withholding. Secondly, it gives the intimacy anorexic a way to be disconnected and less emotionally committed to the real spouse who has flaws as we all do. In *Intimacy Anorexia: The Workbook,* I have anorexic clients write a Thank You and Goodbye Letter to the fantasy person. Below are some comments from anorexics and their spouses about the fantasy person.

Rachel (Spouse): *He has an image in his head and he will not engage in a loving, caring relationship with me.*

Claire (Spouse): *This one is the hardest for me. We can be out to dinner, the movies, Wal-mart, or watching television and he seems to always be looking. When we are at dinner, I've seen him look in a specific direction a lot. I have actually turned around and looked and I can always spot the type he looks at, which is blonde hair for sure. He has to see what each blonde person looks like. He denies it; I know what I see. I've even said, "Is there someone you're looking for?"*

Stephanie (Spouse): *His fantasy girl is NOT like the person he married. It is more of what he was married to before me e.g., tall, athletic, red headed, a little loose acting. I asked why he married me and he says, "...because I couldn't get a model to move to where we live." We live in the sticks of a very poor rural area. I thought it was love; what was I thinking?*

Holly (Spouse): *The intimacy anorexic masturbates to his "dream girl."*

Abby (Spouse): *I tried to always be someone I wasn't...I tried to be his fantasy girl. I couldn't begin to try to win! I tried running, dieting, piercing, and lots of different things for attention.*

Tamara (Spouse): *My husband's fantasy girl is always sexually available to meet every desire he has. She never speaks or has any value as a human being. She worships him and his manhood.*

Sam (Anorexic): *This fantasy was all done in my mind as the perfect relationship of all physical and no emotional needs to meet.*

Fear of Intimacy

Fear is a great friend. It paralyzes your resources and you can justify this because you're afraid. I mean, who can hold you guilty because you're afraid, right? That's the belief that the fear of intimacy gives the intimacy anorexic.

It's okay to be afraid after all, "you have been hurt before by your spouse or others like them. You know it's only a matter of time until you will be hurt again, so stay inside yourself. You know it's not safe, so don't trust, be afraid and sit down." These are actual thoughts the friend of fear of intimacy will offer up to help justify the withholding or pushing away of the spouse to create distance.

You see, now that there is distance, you don't need to be afraid. It's okay, your spouse is effectively pushed away. Fear is a great friend of the anorexic, especially when Fear also brings along The Victim or some of the other friends of intimacy anorexia. In *Intimacy Anorexia: The Workbook,* I have intimacy anorexic's write a Thank You and Goodbye Letter to the fears of intimacy anorexia. Below are some comments from anorexics and their spouses about fear of intimacy.

Rachel (Spouse): *I know that he is terrified of this, I just don't know why and he will not tell me. It scares me because I know there must be something really bad that I don't already know and I know a lot of brutal stuff.*

Virginia (Spouse): *My spouse doesn't share anything unless I ask him and then it feels like I am dragging molasses out of a jar.*

Tanya (Anorexic): *If someone knows my heart, I believed they have the ultimate weapon against me. I have always been punished for letting someone into my heart.*

Alison (Spouse): *We were having once a week dates and using discussion questions that dig rather deep. It went well for several weeks and then he began sabotaging the dates by saying mean things and blaming me, out of the blue, for things and then acting surprised if I got upset.*

Miriam (Spouse): *He says: "'I want to become sexually connected with you, just not today.' 'I'm working towards it; I just need more time.' 'If you'd just waited a few more hours/days, I was going to initiate it.'" He has many, many excuses: headaches, backaches, always too tired, he's angry…*

Safety

The intimacy anorexic has a high demand for safety. This friend, Safety, is one of the closest friends of intimacy anorexia. This friend supports the addiction to withholding by cheering it on with lines like: "I must be absolutely safe before I come out," "It must be a promise that you will never, ever hurt me, see a flaw or criticize me in any way," "I demand safety as a condition to relate." Well, of course, this friend is probably the most delusional of the lot. When you're *drinking* together sometimes you don't realize how crazy the person you're talking to really is.

In the real world, all relationships have pain, all spouses definitely give pain and those are the rules of real life. This friend encourages absolutely unrealistic expectations so the spouse is guaranteed to have repeated failure so the intimacy anorexic can justify withholding and creating pain for them.

Safety is a strong and non rational friend, much like fear of intimacy. The level of emotion that is felt by the anorexic is so primitive it often cannot be rationalized with while it is in the first stage of the heart. This friend may be difficult to address, but when you do as the anorexic, you are able to risk, be hurt, feel pain and above all feel loved with your flaws.

As a spouse, Safety demands cannot be met; they are not supposed to be met. You, as the spouse, are set up to fail so the addiction to withholding can stay in a strengthened position. Really, until this friend is dismantled, you're in for some wild rides of irrational experiences and conversations. In *Intimacy Anorexia: The Workbook,* I have intimacy anorexic's write a Thank You and Goodbye Letter to Safety.

Busyness

The friend of Busyness seems to be around the intimacy anorexic much like that cloud around Pig Pen in the Charlie Brown cartoons. There is always something to do: a home project, television, coach a team, exercise, obsess over golf or a sports team, church, PTA or just simply sit in front of the computer for hours.

Busyness often supports the good person box of the intimacy anorexic. You see, these things are productive, helpful, kind, spiritual and just a good thing to do. Busyness allows the anorexic to stay distracted and take a drink of withholding toward the spouse, intentionally, at the same time. It's like the best of both; I look good and get to withhold. Busyness really assists the intimacy anorexic in their rationalization of avoidance for years or decades at a time.

If you're the spouse of the intimacy anorexic you know when Busyness is around because your spouse isn't around. Even if they are home, it's as if they are not there. They're lost in a book, newspaper or a hundred other things, including all variations of technology, which leaves you with the "I'm alone again in my marriage feeling." Granted, it's nicer than blame, control, or criticism, it's just so lonely when Busyness and your spouse get together. In *Intimacy Anorexia: The Workbook* I also have intimacy anorexic's write a Thank You and Goodbye Letter to Business.

Entitlement

This friend is one of the kingpins, of this rat pack, that the anorexic is hanging out with. Entitlement is pure muscle with a tactic that says, "It's my way or the highway" on its 22 inch arm. This friend is the bouncer of the group. He or she is meaner than any other friend, after all, "I am entitled to push, criticize, yell, make you look stupid, control you because I am important and you have no value to me." These ugly beliefs are what this friend of entitlement is all about. "It's all about me, I'm superior, I won't be questioned, I won't be told what to do" are songs this friend sings to the easily influenced intimacy anorexic.

When this friend is coaching the intimacy anorexic, it becomes unclear who their spouse is. The good person mark is totally off and there is hell to pay. Any mean thing about you, your character, your past, your weakness is all fair game. This gets you back in your rightful place-submitted to the addiction of withholding.

This friend doesn't like to be exposed. If you're the anorexic, you're in for a fight to let this one go. If you're a spouse, don't even engage this one. Your energy makes it grow bigger so leave it alone. You are best to leave or have a plan in place when Entitlement shows up. In *Intimacy Anorexia: The Workbook* I have intimacy anorexic's write a Thank You and Goodbye Letter to Entitlement.

Control

This is the balance of the team, which supports the addiction to withholding, which starves the marriage. Control has to do the tight walk of keeping almost everyone believing the intimacy anorexic is wonderful and keeping a blind eye to the withholding behavior toward the spouse. The need for control is important to most addictions but it is the glue that keeps this addiction to withholding intact.

Without control there would be flaws, authenticness and vulnerability. Control, like a hard wax on a car, fills these cracks and all you have is the great shine everyone loves to love. Control manifests differently for each intimacy anorexic. For some it's money, sex, time, withholding love or praise or just not connecting, but Control holds the fort down. If the anorexic feels his or her image is under attack, Control, along with the bully, anger, will come out and protect the image and secure the parameter.

If the anorexic has been married long or even a few years, the spouse can probably identify this friend, Control. It's this friend that stops the spouse cold in their tracks. It's unbelievably different when this friend finds a new home away from the intimacy anorexia. I often have intimacy anorexic clients write a Thank You and Goodbye Letter to this friend, Control. Below are some comments from anorexics and their spouses about Control.

Rachel (Spouse): *He remains in control at all times. He stays silent until I can't take it anymore (the isolation) and I fall apart and go talk to him.*

Pat (Spouse): *My husband strives to keep all control. He hates there to be any control out of his hands. He liked me much better as a doormat.*

Tanya (Anorexic): *As long as I am in control, no one can hurt me. I cannot control a lot of things, but I can control who I let into who I really am deep down.*

Rose (Anorexic): *I used control to keep myself in what I thought was a "safe" place, but really didn't allow myself to even dare to make the changes I needed to get more healthy.*

Independence

This friend allows the intimacy anorexic to stay in the second stage of development. The first stage of development being dependence which is forced trust, the last stage of development is interdependence which is a choice to trust. These friends say, "no it's better to just take care of themselves, don't trust others, you'll be in debt to them." This can be so severe that they won't' let others help them, not because they don't need the help, but because they don't want to feel indebted or owe that person anything.

Independence is the guy who gives consistent push back when things are getting too close. To trust the spouse is to feel a loss of independence, which can feel like a loss of self to some intimacy anorexics. Independence can also feel like adolescence and rear up with messages of, "don't tell me what to do, nobody tells me what to do. If I wanted another dad or mom I would have married one. Who do you think you are?"

If you're the spouse, independence is that bump in the road just when you thought you were getting along. You were looking forward to a night alone, a significant stretch of quality time and bump, "I'm going to go to X first" creating mild distance allowing the intimacy anorexic to regain their equilibrium of distance. I have my Intimacy anorexic clients write a Thank You and Goodbye Letter to Independence. Below are some comments from anorexics and their spouses about Independence.

Rachel (Spouse): *We have dated for four years and he has no intention of doing anything else. This lets his emotional needs be met without letting me get too much in his space.*

Virginia (Spouse): *My spouse comes and goes as he pleases to his men's meetings without regard for my schedule or our five kids.*

Todd (Anorexic): *My favorite times are when I am alone and I don't need to interact with others.*

Tanya (Anorexic): *I don't need anyone to meet my needs. I can take care of myself.*

Miriam (Spouse): *From the beginning of the marriage, we agreed to join our assets. What I learned; however, is that what this really meant was MY money and assets are OURS but HIS are HIS. My salary goes into the family pool for bills; any income he generates is his to spend for whatever he wants, whenever he wants. We have joint checking/savings account, and he has his own separate, individual one.*

Selfishness

There's not an addict alive that doesn't know selfishness. This friend of the addict is regularly looking out for number one, and in this case it is the intimacy anorexic. This friend makes it difficult to see the team picture and is capitalizing on situations to meet a hypothetical need at best or at worst looking for a way to help the addict withhold having a quick drink.

Selfishness is the jab to the spouse's weak spot, including glares, the rationalization of keeping every commitment, even the commitment to clean the pool but not the commitment to love, honor or cherish the spouse. Selfishness keeps the intimacy anorexic limited on empathy. Since they can't see others, it makes it hard at times to feel the pain of others.

The spouse is very aware of this selfish presence. It's those moments when you feel you have an extra child instead of another adult. It's when you hope the children really don't understand why your spouse is committed to do X, when you were earlier agreeing to do Y, and the only reason is because they don't want to. Intimacy anorexics would do well to write a therapeutic Thank You and Goodbye Letter to Selfishness. Below are some comments from anorexics and their spouses about selfishness.

Rachel (Spouse): *When I talk to him about sexuality being a normal, healthy part of a relationship he just says that he doesn't think it is important. I tell him I do and if he doesn't want it we need to end the relationship so that I can be with someone else and so can he. He says he doesn't want to be with anyone else. I feel crazy.*

Pat (Spouse): *He will eat out or whatever else he wants, but he does not always care if our needs are attended to. He is perfectly fine with solo sex, ignoring all relational needs just as long as he gets what he wants.*

Virginia (Spouse): *My spouse blew off our 21st anniversary (no card, no gift, and no dinner) because he is a teacher and had progress reports due that week. When I had our second miscarriage, my spouse left me crying at the OB's parking lot and went back to work. Then he didn't want to talk about it.*

Todd (Anorexic): *There are certain foods that I buy that are just for me and I get angry when anyone touches them. I rarely share with others.*

Tanya (Spouse): *No one around him has any value or needs. He has needs that must be met or else. His needs are not only the most important, but they are the only needs.*

Rose (Anorexic): *I was very selfish because I couldn't see anyone else's point of view except my own. That is the only way I seemed to know how to survive.*

The Wall

The Wall is probably the friend I often have to explain the most, but after I do, the intimacy anorexic goes "Oh yeah, I got that one too." The wall is like a thick glass that surrounds the intimacy anorexic. Originally it was designed to keep others out but over time it has grown to keep them in. Even when the intimacy anorexic wants to join, connect or even emote they feel stuck, frozen or unavailable. It's like they can see what's going on, and even have the right social queuing to know what would be expected, but they just can't seem to connect the dots. Stuck behind the glass wall they can see and be seen, it just seems that they can't touch or be touched.

The spouse experiences this as frozen moments. The best way to describe it is like a skip in a record. The songs playing, you know the melody and then there is a bump, and the moment is missed or not mutually shared. Within the *Intimacy Anorexia: The Workbook,* I have intimacy anorexic's write a Thank You and Goodbye Letter to The Wall.

The Backdoor

The Backdoor is a faceless friend to those addicted to withholding. It's this friend who just quietly but regularly lets the intimacy anorexic know, "You're not really happy, you'd be happier with someone who is... Really, being alone might even be better. The kids and I would be better without him/her. I don't really know why I stay."

It's this resignation that somehow the intimacy anorexic has resigned to for settling for less. This backdoor is insidious because it allows them, or should I say, gives them permission to not fully accept, fully engage or fully invest in their spouse. The backdoor is that quiet but steady lack of enjoyment of the spouse. This friend makes sure that the intimacy anorexic keeps their spouse's flaws at the forefront of their mind.

The spouse experiences the backdoor as not ever feeling good enough, loved or really often feeling not wanted. It's like somehow you feel you won second or third place and the winner, well, is not available. The winner is the illusive fantasy which keeps the intimacy anorexic from being present and celebrating you. In *Intimacy Anorexia: The Workbook* I have intimacy anorexic's write a Thank You and Goodbye Letter to The Backdoor.

These friends probably have felt eerily familiar at times. No, I have not been videotaping your life. I have, however, spent many years of my career with this addict to withholding. He or she tends to have similar friends.

In recovery, I recommend that they not only write the letters of thank you and goodbye to these friends but also read them out loud and stay aware of these friends so that when they knock at the door of your heart, you don't let them back in.

Recovery, without these friends, is a lot more fun, flexible and appreciative the spouse in your life. Also, when you are sober, you really get to see and experience just how great your spouse is.

9

Recovering Strategies with the Spouse

You might be thinking, Dr. Weiss, shouldn't we be talking about what I need to be doing personally for recovery before I do recovery work with my spouse? Well, you might be right if you were an alcoholic or some other type of an addict. Sobriety from withholding for an anorexic is the active initiating of emotional, spiritual and sexual intimacy toward their spouse.

You may have gone to therapy in the past where the therapist, unfamiliar with anorexia recovery, asked to see you individually. Intimacy anorexics love therapists like this because they don't make them get sober by doing the work of intimacy together with their spouse. That's like never asking the alcoholic to stop drinking and only talking about their family of origin during therapy. It is great to talk about family of origin but the alcoholic must stop drinking to become sober. Likewise, it's great to address individual issues but the intimacy anorexics must get sober by doing intimacy work with their spouse.

The spouse also deserves to know if the anorexic is going to stop withholding after years of this behavior. If the intimacy anorexic completes another year of therapy but doesn't connect, the spouse is now another year more deprived of intimacy with intentional pain in their life. Measuring sobriety can give both of you a clear picture of what the anorexic really wants. Remember, addicts of any kind do what they want whether it's recovery or addictive behaviors.

Rather, start your recovery with your spouse and use your individual recovery, which we will include in the next chapter, to support and fuel your recovery with your spouse. What you do toward and with your spouse determines your sobriety, not insight into why you do something. It's like the food anorexic wanting to talk about anything but the lifting of the spoon and putting food in their mouth.

Three Dailies

The Three Dailies is the core of your intimacy anorexia sobriety. If you, as the intimacy anorexic, do not initiate this exercise, you have relapsed and you did **NOT** have a day of sobriety. Your spouse is to do all these exercises with you; however, they are not to initiate them with you. The only way they would initiate this would be if you are both intimacy anorexic and then you rotate responsibility monthly to make sure you're both sober.

Hear me on this, if you are the spouse of an anorexic, don't initiate these exercises. The intimacy anorexic is like a chick inside an egg, they must push out towards you to heal. Initiating is a big part of their healing, so don't rob them of this important step to grow. If they don't initiate toward you, they don't want to be intimate, they want to be anorexic. You, as a spouse may have to face the real hard truth that your anorexic spouse may not really want intimacy with you. So don't help at all on initiating. You both need the truth of the anorexic's behavior to know the truth about their commitment to their intimacy anorexia recovery.

The anorexic also will need to have consequences for when they don't accomplish this by a certain time of day e.g., 10:00 p.m. If they don't initiate by that time, then they get a consequence e.g., clean bathrooms, two mile run or 30 minute backrub to the spouse. Then, they do the exercises after the consequence that night. Now let's walk through the three daily exercises.

The first of the Three Dailies is the feelings exercise. This exercise will be challenging at first, but it will get easier even in a couple weeks. In the Appendix, you will find a list of feelings. For the first 90 days, randomly put your finger down on the page and do whatever feeling you point to. The intimacy anorexic goes first, then the spouse, then the intimacy anorexic does a second feeling word and lastly the spouse does their second feeling word. Once you pick a feeling put it into these two sentences:

I feel _____ when _____ (This is the present tense).

I first remember feeling _____ when _____ (This example is under the age of 18).

You both pick different words. This exercise will give you both enhanced skills at identifying and communicating emotional intimacy. When you do the exercise with each other, make sure you follow these three simple rules to keep the exercise safe for both of you.

Rule #1: No examples ever about your spouse or the marriage during the exercise.

Rule #2: Maintain eye contact during the exercise.

Rule #3: No feedback when someone shares a feeling, just listen to them.

You will do the feelings exercise just this way daily for 90 days, then you will just do two feelings with each other from that particular day until death do you part!

You see, intimacy anorexia, by definition, is active withholding of emotional intimacy. As you do this intentional communicating of feelings from your heart to each other you are moving toward sobriety.

Some intimacy anorexics are more committed to the addiction than they are to their marriage or recovery. This addict will do everything he or she can to sabotage this feelings exercise and the other exercises in this chapter. Here's what sabotaging looks like.

1. Just not initiating

2. Making excuses to not do the consequence agreed upon

3. Being trite or trivial during exercises

4. Doing it with their head only, not intentionally engaging you with their heart

5. Creating pain for the spouse in the exercise by not looking at them or talking at them and not to them.

If you see these behaviors, the addict is negotiating on how little they can recover and keep the image of the marriage. This is the alcoholic saying how little they can drink. As an alcoholic, you can't drink, as an anorexic you can't withhold because that is the addiction.

The second exercise also has to do with emotionally connecting with your spouse. One of the characteristics of intimacy anorexia is criticism; focusing on the flaws of your spouse. Another characteristic is withholding praise in intimacy anorexia. In this exercise we give two compliments or praises to each other. This is an exercise where you both think of two things you love, like or appreciate about each other. The intimacy anorexic goes first with eye contact and tells their spouse, "<u>Name</u>, I really <u>love, like, appreciate</u> (pick one) _____ about you." The next step is important. When the spouse lets it into their heart, they are to say, "Thank you". This is a receipt back to their spouse for the praise that was given to them. Then the spouse gives a praise and the intimacy anorexic says, "Thank you." This repeats with another praise. Like a ping pong ball going back and forth, each will do two praises toward the other.

The third exercise is praying together. This isn't a matter of faith, it's a matter of recovery. Regardless of your beliefs, you both pray out loud together. Remember, by definition, intimacy anorexia includes a spiritual withholding from the spouse. This piece is essential for the intimacy anorexic, or any addict for that matter, to heal. So, the intimacy anorexic prays out loud and then the spouse prays out loud.

Like the feelings exercise, it may be awkward for a couple of weeks, but then it becomes comfortable and desired. So make sure these three exercises are completed daily. I would also recommend that you keep track of the consistency so you both can see the level of sobriety or addiction to withholding that you are both living in. Let's recap.

3 Dailies

- 2 Feelings each
- 2 Praises each
- 1 Pray each
- Establish a daily time
- Establish a consequence if the intimacy anorexic does not initiate these exercises
- Monitor sabotaging behavior

Sexual Agreement

A sexual agreement is the next step of this three leg recovery stool. By definition, the intimacy anorexic is addicted to withholding emotional, spiritual and yes, sexual intimacy. Remember, we are going for connectedness during sex. Like some may sabotage the feelings exercise, you may also see those same behaviors around sex. If the anorexic is trying to sabotage the sexual agreement exercise, the behaviors you might find would be as follows.

1. Not keeping their commitment to have sex
2. Disconnecting during sex
3. Not following through with consequences
4. Using an anorexic characteristic to make the spouse not desire sex
5. Negative communication before, during, or after sex

Sad to say, some intimacy anorexics are married to withholding, not to the spouse. This commitment to the addiction of withholding will definitely show up if you see these sabotaging behaviors toward the sexual agreement.

There are three components to a sexual agreement. First, establish a weekly frequency. I really recommend no less than one time a week. On average if you're under 50, 2-3 times a week would be average and if you're over 50, 1-2 times a week would be average. Once you establish a frequency you go to step two in the sexual agreement.

Now that both of you have established a desired sexual frequency, next is to create how this frequency will be accomplished on a weekly basis. You can just, 1) pick days, 2) split the week into parts or rotate days or weeks back and forth. In a split week one person gets to initiate on Sunday, Monday, Tuesday. Wednesday can be anybodies day or nobody's day depending on the frequency you both agree to. Then the other person initiates on Thursday, Friday, and Saturday. This method can accommodate 2-3 times sexually a week for the couple. The rotating of days goes like this. Each person gets up to 3 days to initiate. If it's my day one and I don't initiate, it's okay. Day two I initiate and then the next day becomes my spouse's day one and back and forth like that. So I can initiate any of the three days, but when I initiate, the next day becomes my spouses turn to initiate.

In the rotation of weeks, one person gets weeks one and three. The second person gets weeks two and four. You both initiate the frequency you agreed to and rotate the weeks for who initiates sex.

Let me take a moment to talk about initiating and if this is difficult to understand, see the exercises in the intimacy anorexia workbook. If the intimacy anorexic rarely initiates sex, then for the first 60 days the intimacy anorexic does all the initiating of sex. If both are intimacy anorexics then flip a coin on who does month one and who does 100% of month two. If your both keeping your sexual word, then go to a mutual initiating system.

If the spouse is okay to initiate immediately half the time, great! However, if the intimacy anorexic is slacking and not doing consequences, get professional help. The third part of a sexual agreement is setting up consequences if someone doesn't ask, someone says no, negotiating expectations about menstrual cycle is also important so everybody is on the same page regarding this monthly issue.

Each person sets up their own consequences for not keeping their sexual agreements. For the intimacy anorexic, especially if this is a key way they intentionally create pain for the spouse, the consequence needs to be extremely severe. Some anorexics have had set consequences like:

- Half day wage to political party they don't vote for.
- Sleep in the garage with only a blanket
- Cook for a week
- Give wife $200 to go to the spa or husband $200 toward something
- Take off a day of work and just be with their spouse
- One month no television or computer

Any consequence will do; it just needs to be painful for the anorexic. This sexual withholding is probably the meanest, cruelest and most intentional of all the anorexic characteristics. Any intimacy anorexic that won't give themselves to their spouse, is not sober.

Recovery, as an intimacy anorexic, has two core behaviors. Firstly, do your Three Dailies; secondly, keep your sexual agreement. This is the basics of intimacy anorexia recovery as far as with your spouse. In the *Intimacy Anorexia: The Workbook* there's many other exercises you can do to expedite your intimacy anorexia recovery.

Life is too short to be addicted to anything. As you travel this road of recovery, you will be experiencing intimacy (emotionally, spiritually and sexually) like never before. You can be one of those couples I see with big smiles on their faces-not believing how much they really do love each other. That picture is worth all the work it takes to achieve that loving feeling again. Intimacy anorexia is something that can go in remission and when it does you both can feel loved again.

10

Recovering Self

In this chapter, I want to share with you a handful of the early exercises for intimacy anorexia recovery. I want to first introduce you to what has come to be known as the "5 C's", which is short for the five commandments. These are five exercises that you do daily (except for the meetings) for the first 90 days of recovery. Within *Intimacy Anorexia: The Workbook,* there is a form to track your success during the first 90 days of recovery. I find that tracking your recovery is a really good idea so that you have something to measure your perspective. These five commandments have helped many on the road to recovery and, if applied, I am confident they can be of help to you as well.

Commandment #1: Pray

Regardless of your faith or lack thereof, when you get up or even before you hit the floor with your feet out of bed, ask God to help you in your recovery today. This prayer might be as simple as, "God, help me give love to my spouse, keep my heart open as I heal, and any help you can offer would be great." Some of you are already familiar with prayer. Just keep it connecting and honest, not a memorized prayer that you repeat without feeling. This prayer is just you opening up your heart to God and asking for some help on the road to recovery today.

Commandment #2: Read

If you are reading this chapter, then you are already doing Commandment #2 which is to read recovery literature about intimacy anorexia. There isn't really much more available, at the time of this writing, about intimacy anorexia. Here are a couple of other ideas. Firstly, almost any book on marriage or intimacy would do. There are two books I often recommend for intimacy anorexics to read, both by the Arbinger Institute: *Leadership and Self Deception* and *Anatomy of Peace*. These would be good follow-up books to the book you are now reading. Read daily to stay focused on your goal to actively initiate emotional, spiritual and sexual intimacy with your spouse.

Commandment #3: Meetings

Since intimacy anorexia is the youngest member to the Twelve Step family, its groups are few and far between. You can call Heart to Heart Counseling Center at 719-278-3708 for a national directory for Intimacy Anorexia Groups. If you start a group or know of one, please let us know so we can refer intimacy anorexics to your group. See the Appendix of this book for the group structure if you would like to start a group.

If there are no groups in your immediate area, then I highly recommend the therapist led telephone support groups. These are led by therapists trained through AASAT (American Association for Sex Addiction Therapy). This is the only organization that is training therapists to treat intimacy anorexia.

To attend a telephone group, you simply call in at the time of the group. The group consists of 6-8 members who are also intimacy anorexics. We have separate groups for women and men. During the group, the group members cover the workbook exercises that were completed that week from *Intimacy Anorexia: The Workbook* and *Intimacy Anorexia: The Steps* workbooks. You give each other feedback and there is a topic for each group. This becomes your team to help you get and stay free from the addiction to withholding from your spouse.

Commandment #4: Phone Calls

Members of a group call each other daily for the first 90 days to check in on: 1. progress of initiating the 3 Dailies and sex, and 2. any acting in or withholding characteristics (the 10) or other specific strategies you identified that you're working on. Both members share and support each other.

Initiating a call can be difficult at first for intimacy anorexics but again within a two week period you are over this struggle. Recovery from any addiction is a team sport. You cannot make it by yourself (remember, you tried that already). These calls can be a real lifesaver, especially if you're spiraling into patterns of withholding. You can get grounded, take responsibility, and move toward your spouse and not away from them.

Commandment #5: Pray Again

Any day sober beats a day of withholding. Take a moment and thank God for a sober day. He deserves thanks for helping you have the miracle of recovery in initiating intimacy toward your spouse.

To review, the 5 C's to recovery are:

- Pray
- Read
- Meetings
- Calls
- Pray Again

Affirmations

I find that with intimacy anorexics, like any addicts, have faulty thinking patterns. In the recovering community they call this "stinking thinking." These negative and not helpful thoughts about yourself and toward your spouse can be a limitation in your recovery.

For the first 90 days of recovery it's a good idea to do these affirmations to give yourself a second intentional template to respond from other than the one you created within your addiction.

An affirmation is a present, positive statement that is spoken out loud daily while in a relaxed state. This is done daily for at least 90 days. This relaxed state allows the "new software" to be placed into your core belief system. Creating a new template is very important since it is these core beliefs about oneself and others that keeps the anorexic from experiencing true intimacy.

How to do affirmations:

1. Make a list of affirmations (refer to the following page for examples).
2. Get into a relaxed position (sofa, bed, or chair) during a time when you are not planning to sleep.
3. Relax your body e.g., feel your feet relax, then calves, legs, etc. Make sure your whole body is relaxed before proceeding.
4. Take your list of affirmations and read them out loud.

It is not important that you believe each statement to complete this exercise. In time, you will be able to believe these truths about yourself and your spouse.

- I am a loveable person.
- I am able to experience my feelings today.
- I give myself permission to share my feelings with my spouse today.
- I give myself permission to share myself with my spouse.
- I have value.
- My spouse also has value.
- I am a sexual person.
- My spouse is a sexual person.
- I give myself permission to feel sexual toward my spouse today.
- I give myself permission to ask my spouse for sexual intimacy today.
- I can trust myself.
- I can trust my spouse.
- I am an intelligent person.
- My spouse is an intelligent person.
- If I feel anger, I can talk about it directly.
- If I feel emotional pain, I give myself permission to talk to a safe person about it.

- Today, I can be free from withholding love, sex or money from my spouse.
- I can celebrate my spouse today with love, sex, money or time.
- I am sexual.
- As a part of who I am, I embrace my sexuality.
- I can learn to know my spouse today.
- Today I can allow my spouse know me.

Now, I want to add another set of affirmations for those of you who really have your spouse in the bad or Darth Vader box regularly. Do the same process as far as relaxing and reading statements. Again these statements are present and positively directed at your spouse. Do these for 90 days and you could see an entirely new spouse.

- My spouse is on my side.
- My spouse is my biggest cheerleader.
- My spouse's perceptions are possible and need to be heard.
- I give my spouse my heart today.
- Today I respect my spouse.

Treatment

If you want therapy, and that is a really good idea, I would suggest a therapist who understands intimacy anorexia. If you go to a therapist who allows you to gripe about your spouse and actually encourages your friendships with the victim, blame and selfishness, then you're in the wrong office. You don't need pity. You need, like any addict, to take responsibility.

I really recommend phone sessions (or local sessions, if available) with an AASAT trained therapist. I also recommend the phone groups as a part of intimacy anorexia treatment.

Heart to Heart Counseling Center offers 3-Day Intensives for couples with intimacy anorexia. This is a great jump start for your recovery. You can identify the cause for the intimacy anorexia, do exercises, go to local groups and your spouse gets to work through significant residual from being in a relationship with an anorexic. Heart to Heart Counseling Center also has groups to help process the healing. If both spouses are intimacy anorexics, you can both start and accelerate your recovery by attending a 3-Day Intensive. For more information, call 719-278-3708.

Lastly, I can't reiterate enough how much the materials, *Intimacy Anorexia: The Workbook* and *Intimacy Anorexia: The Steps,* can help. Workbooks like these have been used effectively to help you make progress one page at a time.

You deserve a life in recovery. You have to work for recovery but if you think about it, you have to work at being anorexic. So choose to work toward recovery. The miracle is absolutely amazing and your spouse deserves to be connected to and celebrated.

Factors in Recovery

The following are road markers to know if you are actually in recovery. These are short ideas but can be a quick checklist to go through periodically to make sure you're driving down the right road.

1. Addicts Do What They Want to Do

Addicts of all kinds do not lack motivation. Self will is the problem. Addicts do exactly what they want to do even if it is being self destructive. Nobody can stop the addict. This is a rule of thumb I apply to addicts. Watch what they are doing and you'll know what they want.

2. Believe Behavior

Addicts can talk a really good game. They have what I call verbal reality. If they say it, it is true; if they say it with emotional vibrato, it is really true. However, they don't feel obligated to have to follow through. If you take the first principle I mentioned, addicts do what they want to do. Today, they are doing what they want. If they are doing the recovery exercises and trying to connect with their spouse, then they want to be sober from the addiction to withholding that is killing their marriage. If they are doing things half heartedly, then they are negotiating for as little change as possible. If they are not doing any recovery work, then the addict doesn't really want his or her spouse. Since the anorexic doesn't want to look bad and file for divorce, he or she will intentionally create pain for the spouse.

3. Creativity

I just told you addicts of all kinds are self motivated. If addicts want to do something, they don't need goading to get something done, they just do it. One of the ways I can determine if an intimacy anorexic is in recovery is by following their creativity. Are they being creative when their schedule changes so that they can get the 3 dailies done? Are they keeping their sexual agreement and calling their group members or is their creativity being used for excuse making and avoiding responsibility to get sober by intentionally creating pain for their spouse? You may have heard the phrase, "follow the money" with addicts and you'll know the truth. For intimacy anorexics it's, "follow the creativity" and you'll know the truth.

4. Groups and Calls

Since initiating intimacy is difficult, I know intimacy anorexics that are making their calls daily and attending groups are really stretching themselves. These two behaviors tell me a lot about whether the anorexic is going to do what it takes or what is comfortable for them. In the midst of their addiction, they chose their safety and comfort zone over their spouse thousands of times. If I still see this choice consistently, in regards to group and calls, they are stuck.

Honesty About Relapses

If an addict is honest about slips, we are still making progress. This is especially true of the intimacy anorexic. Remember, sharing flaws is hard, and if they are doing that hard work, it is definitely positive! If an intimacy anorexic can stop and say, "Forgive me, I was acting in or withholding by doing X" we are in good shape. If their spouse is still spending a lot of time convincing the intimacy anorexic that they are withholding, then that is a sign of dishonesty which supports denial of an addiction rather than recovery from one.

Quick to do Consequences

When an intimacy anorexic finds themselves acting in, withholding, pushing away, doesn't follow their sexual agreement and doesn't do The Three Dailies but has a set of consequences and does them quickly, without complaining then this is also a positive sign. However, if they won't do them, and continues to sulk or whine, that's not a positive direction. If they refuse to do their recovery work then they are actively in their addiction mode and nobody can tell them what to do. In recovery we call this King or Queen Baby.

Emotional Thawing

This is not something an addict can fake. If they are doing their work, they begin to emotionally thaw out. They will feel more feelings and feel them more intensely. It will feel as if they are really experiencing life emotionally. I see this thawing out by the 90 day period. If you don't see this, there may be intimacy anorexia drinking going on while maintaining the emotional frozen or limited state.

Leaning Toward

Lastly, a specific behavior I see with intimacy anorexics in recovery is what I call leaning toward. In anorexia, when the intimacy anorexic gets hurt, they pull or push away and sometimes both in the acting in of their anorexia.

When pain or conflict comes up with the spouse, they can stay in it and actually move toward the spouse to resolve the issue and not lose the connection. Staying in the forward position for someone who recoiled most of their marriage is on the road in the right direction. This is a real sign that recovery is occurring for him or her.

I hope you periodically look at these factors in recovery for yourself to prevent going the wrong way too long or see how steady you are driving on the road of recovery.

11

The Twelve-Steps

Here we will enter into the recovery program known as the Twelve Steps. The original Twelve Steps were written many years ago for *Alcoholics Anonymous*. These alcoholics, after some period of sobriety, decided to write down the principles and the steps they took to maintain their sobriety and to live a healthier life. These principles and steps have been used throughout the world to help millions of people with various addictions such as narcotic abuse, overeating, emotional problems, co-dependency, sexual addiction and now intimacy anorexia. Here, they are adapted for intimacy anorexics.

The Twelve-Steps of Alcoholics Anonymous Adapted for Intimacy Anorexics

1.   We admitted we were powerless over our intimacy anorexia, and that our lives had become unmanageable.

2. Came to believe that a power greater than our selves could restore us to sanity.

3. Made a decision to turn our will and our lives over to the care of God, as we understood God.

4. Made a searching and fearless moral inventory of ourselves.

5. Admitted to God, to ourselves, and to another human being the exact nature of our wrongs.

6. Were entirely ready to have God remove all these defects of character.

7. Humbly asked God to remove our shortcomings.

8. Made a list of all persons we had harmed and became willing to make amends to them all.

9. Made direct amends to such people wherever possible, except when to do so would injure them or others.

10. Continued to take personal inventory, and when we were wrong, promptly admitted it.

11. Sought through prayer and meditation to improve our conscious contact with God as we understood God, praying only for knowledge of God's will for us and the power to carry that out.

12. Having had a spiritual awakening as the result of these steps, we tried to carry this message to others, and to practice these principles in all our day to day living.

Note: The Twelve-Steps are reprinted and adapted with permission of Alcoholics Anonymous World Services, Inc. Permission to reprint and adapt the Twelve Steps does not mean that AA has reviewed or approved the content of this publication, nor that AA agrees with the views expressed herein. AA is a program of recovery from alcoholism. Use of the Twelve Steps, in connection with programs and activities patterned after AA, addresses other problems, not otherwise implied.

An Interpretation of the Twelve-Steps for Intimacy Anorexics

What we will attempt to do in the following pages is to explain the principles and concepts of the Twelve-Steps as they are used for recovery from intimacy anorexia, so that you can implement them in your personal recovery. Our comments here should not be construed as representing any particular Twelve-Step fellowship. They are my own interpretation of the steps from my own experience, as well as from more than twenty years of clinical experience helping addicts of all types recover by utilizing the Twelve-Step process. In the following pages I will be addressing the twelve steps for the anorexics.

Step One: We admitted we were powerless over our intimacy anorexia and that our lives had become unmanageable.

We. I am so glad that the first word in the first step is "we." Anyone would hate to think that they were the only person who ever went through this. Intimacy anorexia is an international as well as a national problem. "We" means that we have similar experiences and we are alike. We grew up in the same family thousands of miles apart. *We* is a comforting word in this step. You can see that you are not alone and don't have to be alone. You can get better if you decide to get together with others. *We* is an encouraging word and is also essential. Without each other, we often fail to recover.

Admitted. This is a difficult word. Many of us have had situations in our childhood that we have had to admit. Maybe we stole something or something happened to us and we had to admit what we did. Remember those feelings of dread before admitting something? Then we went ahead and admitted it. We told what we did or what happened to us. After we admitted it, we felt less heavy or burdened and as if we could now move on. Admitting for the intimacy anorexic is one of the hardest things we will do in our recovery. Admitting is a very important aspect of recovery and only those who admit to intimacy anorexia can move forward in recovery and life.

We Were Powerless. Again, I'm glad that there is a "we" in there and that I'm not the only one who is powerless. When we talk about power, we talk about control. Authority, strength or force gives us the ability to be over someone else. But that is not what this word is. This word is powerless and as we know, the suffix "less" means without—such as jobless. This is a tough reality for every addict. We are without any strength, power, control or force to influence our addiction to withholding. This is why we need each other and a recovery program. Sometimes that is why we need therapy. We are powerless. We have tried not to withhold without success.

Intimacy Anorexia. The intimacy anorexic is a complicated being. Anorexics withhold creating intentional pain for their spouse and themselves. They withhold, withdraw and push away to stay disconnected. This is a soul in pain. Whatever the reason, the addiction to withholding from their spouse is real, powerful and cunning, like all other addictions.

And That Our Lives. Our lives can be many things. It can be our physical, emotional, intellectual or spiritual life. If you look at all the parts of our lives, they wouldn't equal the totality of our lives. Our lives are the very core of us. It is the inner part of us that identifies us as being separate from another person. This is what has been affected as we look at our intimacy anorexia. This is the part that feels disconnected, alone, confused and isolated when needs are not being met. It is this part of us that allows us to admit something very important.

Had Become. These two words indicate to me that this has taken a while. It means that it took time, energy, process and choices. It didn't just happen. It took a while and then, eventually, it was made. Your life didn't become overwhelming or devastated instantly, but over a period of time.

Unmanageable. When we think about manageable, we think about things being in order or serene. We can tell when we walk into a store whether the store is manageable or unmanageable. This word means unorganized and chaotic. If someone came from the outside and saw this, they would say "What a mess!" Sometimes this is the way we feel, and our feelings can be valid. Our lives in many of the areas we have talked about have become unmanageable, unconnected, uncontrollable, and unpredictable. No matter how hard we have tried to make them look good or perfect, they don't and they are not. Our lives have become empty and hollow in many respects. Now, through Step One, if we can admit this unmanageability, we have a strong hope of recovery.

I encourage everyone to take Step One seriously because it is the foundation of the Twelve Step program. It will cause you to have a good house of recovery to live in for the future.

For further in-depth step work on Step One and all of the Twelve-Steps for Intimacy Anorexics, I encourage you to use *Intimacy Anorexia: The Steps.* This guide is specifically for intimacy anorexics to work through. Each step maximizes recovery, and can aid you in your recovery from withholding from your spouse.

Step Two: *Came to believe that a power greater than ourselves could restore us to sanity*.

Came to Believe. Again, notice the step is written in the past tense. The original steps were written to share the process that the original members of AA went through in recovery. There was a process through which they came to believe.

It is really a simple process. You come to believe many things during your lifetime. For example, you came to believe that there was a Santa Claus. Later you came to believe that there wasn't a Santa Claus. As you grew older, you may have come to believe that a certain person liked you, and later realized they didn't like you. We come to believe certain religious and political positions. There is some consistency to this process throughout our lives. In this process, there is a definite point at which you understand or come to believe.

In Twelve Step groups, the process of coming to believe is something that often happens as a result of exposure to other recovering people. You may not necessarily know the date or the hour when you did come to believe, but you know that you feel differently, and you begin to have hope. This is so important in recovery, because knowing that you have come to believe, or knowing you do believe can save your life. Intimacy anorexics can get down, feel hopeless or worthless, experience severe shame and guilt from past traumas or present circumstances, and resort to sad behaviors of destruction, isolation and withholding from their spouse. Coming to believe can bring hope back into any addict's sails.

A Power. "A" is a common word. You use it every day. A cat, a dog, a book—and in every context in which it is used, it denotes one. If you were going to use a word to describe more than one, you would say "these," or another word that indicates plurality. This step is not written in the plural. It says "a" power greater than ourselves. This is significant. Being an "a" here, you realize that there is one entity, one strength, one energy, one spirit, one power. It is significant that as you come to believe, you also believe in one.

Greater Than Ourselves. This is one of the first areas which require trust from the intimacy anorexic. We now know that there is one that is greater than ourselves. This is the best news we have in recovery; that we don't have to figure this out alone. As you begin to trust this power, you begin to recover from the patterns and poor choices that have been so much a part of your past.

In the original context of AA, this power greater than ourselves indicated that the power was greater than that first group of recovering alcoholics. This one single power was greater than a whole group. That's a lot of power. People in recovery frequently, first recognize this power in the group, but in reality it is greater than the group. Even if you had a power greater than yourself, you may have had difficulty accessing the resources of that power and applying them to your life. In the program, you come to believe that this power has more ability to solve life's problems than you do individually. What a relief!

Could. "Could" is one of the most helpful, loving expressions in the Twelve-Steps. Could this power have the ability, the resources, the energy, the intention of helping you along in the recovery process? It is possible now to begin to be restored. It is possible now to begin to be healthy, to have loving relationships with loving people, to be loved and nurtured in a healthy way. It can be done, and this power can do it. It is the experience of many, in intimacy anorexia recovery, that if given the freedom and the opportunity—in other words if you quit trying to do it all on your own—this power will do for you what you have been unable or unwilling to do for yourself. All you have to do is ask.

Restore Us to Sanity. "Restore" means bringing something back. Frequently when you think of restoration, you think of restoring an automobile or an old house, and making it look like new. The same is true of intimacy anorexia recovery.

Intimacy anorexics have for so long been robbed of spirituality, intimacy, trust, and even their own reality. In a world that should have been safe, we violated ourselves again and again.

Insanity is natural when you live with a disease as crazy as intimacy anorexia. You may have difficulty applying the idea of insanity to yourself, but often having a great spouse and intentionally starving them doesn't seem logical. You try again and again to do something that should work, but doesn't. You try and try to fix the problems that intimacy anorexia creates in your life without success.

The behaviors themselves are insane, but the fact that you use them again and again, never stopping to realize that they're not working, qualifies you to be restored to sanity. It is possible for intimacy anorexics to be restored to sanity. Those already in recovery have experienced it. They are living proof that it is possible to make better choices, and we hope, as you read this, you know that it is possible for you. You may still feel crazy, but if you have gotten this far in your recovery, you have a good chance at finding sanity.

Step Three: *Made a decision to turn our wills and our lives over to the care of God, as we understood God*.

Made. "Made" is kind of like "became." It indicates a process which involves time and choices, but there is definitely a time when it is done. For example, when kids in school make an ashtray, or a meal in home economics, or a dress, there is a time when it is in the process of being made, and then it is completed. It is made. "Made" is something that has been coming along, but is finally resolved to the point that you can say it is done.

A. Here again we come to that little word, "a." It is one. What we are discussing in Step Three is a onetime event. Many people want to spread this step out, but as you move along in this process of working the steps, you will see why we only make this decision one time.

Decision. When you make a decision, you list the good and the bad, the pros and cons of a situation. In this step, you can make a list of what you have done with your life in the past, and how you could deal with your life differently in the future. Such a list makes it easier to make the decision you are asked to make in Step Three. It is a decision.

Compare it to a traditional courtship and marriage. It is like you had an engagement period in Step Two, where you made a commitment to share your life with God. You just have a single ceremony, but it sets the stage for further development through the relationship. Step Three asks you to be willing to share your life with God. The decision is a one time event, but it provides a means for further growth.

To Turn. Turning can be expressed in many ways. Someone said once that turning means "to flip over," kind of like a hot cake. The hot cake gets done on one side, and then you have to turn it over.

It is a pretty simple definition of turn, but it is also pretty profound. If you flip over, you make a total turn or change from the way you have been up to this point.

"Turn" is used on highways all over the world to indicate direction: signs may indicate a left or right turn, or U-turn. When you make a U-turn, you turn around and go in the opposite direction. What you do in Step Three is definitely a U-turn! You turn away from your limited understanding of how life should be. You leave behind perceptions, experiences, and ideas about things you thought you understood. You turn from them and gain a whole new perspective. This is an essential part of recovery. You are turning into something, or turning somewhere else, and it is amazing how far that turn can take you, as you continue in your recovery efforts.

Our Will. Again, this is plural, as the group stays and works together. In this group of safe people, who have turned their wills and lives over to God, you will begin to see this decision as a possibility for yourself. But what is your will? The simplest definition of "will" is probably the ability to make the choices you do for your life. In the group, you will begin to turn over the choices that you make to God. This can be an easy thing for some, but for others it can be a very hard thing to do. It means you must turn your choices over to God, try to understand God's perspective, and follow that perspective in your life. That is why Step Three is so powerful.

As I have mentioned before, in many recovery groups there is a phrase called "stinking thinking." Stinking thinking is the way an addict, alcoholic or a non-recovering person thinks. This thinking doesn't work. The choices non-recovering people make don't bring about positive results. There seems to be certain self-destructiveness to their choices and behavior. Step Three cuts to the core of stinking thinking. It is the beginning of a new life-style.

Giving up their wills is a safety valve for intimacy anorexics. In making decisions about relationships, they are now able to turn to God. As they do, God will demonstrate new directions they can take, and new choices they can make. They will begin getting answers, and will be able to make different choices about their withholding behavior. This is a freedom that is only gained by letting go of their own will, or choices.

Our Lives. Our lives are the result of all our choices. For each individual, life is the totality of all parts. When you turn it all over—spiritually, emotionally, physically, socially, financially and sexually—you give yourself to God. You begin to trust God. You begin to believe that God will take care of you.

You may say this is frightening. "How can I trust God?!" But simply look at what you have trusted in the past. You have trusted your own ability to think, your own ability to make choices. You have taken the advice of a few chosen people who have not necessarily acted in your best interests.

Turning your will and life over is necessary. It is through this trust experience with God that you begin to believe that God loves you. You begin once again to trust yourself. Eventually, you can even regain your trust in people. Step Three is an essential part of working the steps. It is not a luxury. It is necessary for a healthy, happy life. Working the steps is not always easy, and often you do not understand why you must work them. Often the steps are understood only after they have been completed. Then you realize the beauty of this spiritual process, and open yourself to further growth and joy as you walk this road with others who are making the same steps toward recovery.

The Care of God. What do you think of when you hear the word "care?" It is often expressed in terms of someone who loves you, someone who demonstrates some kindness toward you, someone who is willing to get involved in your life, willing to get in there and be patient with you to work with you and not condemn you in the process; someone who can be nurturing. All these pictures of a loving parent or a loving friend can represent care. Care is felt in the release of energy from one person to another, usually through kind behaviors, like providing a listening ear or some other sign of concern.

How does this relate to God? What is the care of God? It is simply God's willingness to be involved in a nurturing, supportive, accepting way in your life. God is concerned for intimacy anorexics. God's concern for others in this world demonstrates that care. You can sometimes see it more clearly in the lives of others than you can in your own life. For some intimacy anorexics, the group is a manifestation of the care of God in their lives. It is possible, by looking at others in your support group to connect with, that it radically changes your life. Something as simple as their support can be seen as the extension of God's care and concern.

Now, we'll talk about God. The original writers of the Twelve-Steps changed only one word from the initial version. In Step Two they changed the word "God" to "a Power greater than ourselves." That is the only change they made, and it was made for this reason: Those first alcoholics said that God was too scary for the recovering person in Step Two. Maybe the recovering person had too many hurts or too many problems with God. This change gives the newcomer an engagement period, and allows them to experience God through the group's care, nurturing and love. In this way, they could come to believe in a caring God who could, and would, help them.

But who is God? Let me share my thoughts with you on this subject. Simply put, God is Love. God is also in authority or in control, especially for those who turn their lives and will over to Him, and switch the authority from themselves to God.

According to what you have learned so far in the steps, God has the ability to restore you. God is more powerful than you are alone, or in a group. God is one who gets actively involved in your life, who has more power and more success than you in dealing with intimacy anorexia. This God can and will help you as you work the Twelve-Steps.

For many, this understanding of God will develop into a faith that is common in the American culture, and will enable the recovering intimacy anorexic to enjoy the benefits of finding a community that shares the same faith.

Some will not. It is a universal blessing of this program. They will come to a greater relationship with God, if they are willing, because God is willing.

The people who have turned their wills and lives over to the care of a God they understand—who have turned their choices over to God—often have more understanding of how God works and how God thinks. The group is a good resource, especially for those early in recovery who want an understanding of God. It is very important to realize, as it pertains to understanding God, that no single person is going to understand the totality of God, but the members of your support group can be helpful in this journey.

As We Understood God. One way to interpret this is to compare your understanding of God with the way you function in relationships with people, because we are talking about a relationship. When you first meet someone, your knowledge of them is limited. Only through time, communication, and commitment to any relationship, do you really come to understand another person. The same is true in your relationship with God. Coming to understand God is a process which is available to any and all in recovery who are willing to turn their wills and lives over. This is so that they can experience a new life, a new freedom, and find happiness. The beauty of finding God in the Twelve-Steps is that as you grow, your understanding of God grows too.

Step Four: Made a searching and fearless moral inventory of ourselves.

Made A Searching. Searching holds the possibility of fun, but for intimacy anorexics, searching can be extremely painful. When you search, you intend to find something. For example, when you lose your keys, you go searching with the intent of finding the keys. As you begin your search inventory, you are searching. You are scrutinizing; you are seeking with intent to find something that is quite significant.

In this context, "searching" indicates that you will have to expend some energy. This is the beginning of what is often referred to in the program as the "action steps." You now begin to take action on your own behalf. Note that this step is also in the past tense. As you begin your inventory, you can know that others have passed this way before, and have survived and gotten better. You are not alone.

Fearless. "Fearless" simply means without fear. This is the attitude with which you approach your moral inventory. Being fearless allows you to view your inventory objectively as you uncover the pain. You will be looking at what was done to you, and what you have done to yourself and others.

Many of the experiences you will be looking at are extremely painful. For some, the painful experience was childhood sexual abuse, for others it was forced oral sex or rape. For some, it will be something they would much rather not ever remember, something they may think they only imagined. Fearlessness will lead you to look at your own part in the sick relationships you have been in as an adult, and at the patterns that have been repeated over and over in your life. You need to look at these things with an attitude of courage and bravery. You can, because in Step Three you turned your will and life over to the care of a loving God.

Moral. "Moral" can be defined as right and wrong, categories of black and white, or good and bad. Something that is immoral could be defined as something that violates your conscience. As you look at your life in Step Four, you will be looking for things that you've done that have violated your conscience. For example, as children, many of us were not supposed to get a cookie. There might not be anything wrong with having a cookie, but we were told not to, so it became wrong. Yet we waited until our parents could not see, and took a cookie anyway. It probably tasted good, but we may have felt badly afterward. We felt badly because we knew we did something wrong.

In Step Four, you will also be looking at how you were violated by others. Have you ever said to yourself, "If they really knew me, they wouldn't like me. If they knew I was sexually abused or raped, they wouldn't be my friend"? The shame and guilt you carry from the actions of other people toward you can be overwhelming. Step Four is designed to release you from that shame and guilt as you look at how your moral code has been violated by others.

It is wrong to believe that you are unworthy because of your past. In recovery, you come to know yourself and let others know you. Step Four is about coming to know yourself, being honest with yourself about what happened, taking into account how it affected your life, and where it leaves you today. In short, Step Four is an inventory. You will list everything that happened, even if it involved others and you were simply an innocent bystander—as in the case of the divorce of parents, or the death of a grandparent or other significant family member. Such an event may not have had anything to do with your morals, but it did affect you emotionally.

Inventory. What are you to inventory in Step Four? You inventory your experiences because, as a human being, that is what you have on hand. You inventory your memory, for that is what you have been given to record your experiences. Many see this inventory as a life story. It is a process where you begin to see the truth of what you've done, and what has been done to you. Some things will be negative, others will be positive. When a storekeeper takes inventory, he lists not only the things he wants to get rid of, but the things he wants to keep. And he doesn't just make a mental note of it—he writes it down.

Step Four is a written assignment. You will need to have pen or pencil, paper, and a quiet place where you can be uninterrupted. Some just begin writing. Some organize their inventory by ages, such as zero-to six years, seven to twelve years, and so on. Still others have done it by first listing all the traumatic events they can remember—things that were done to them or by them that violated their value system— and then writing how they felt at the time, and how they feel now about those events. There is no right or wrong way to write an inventory. The important thing is just to do it. You will be face to face for perhaps the first time with the total reality of your life.

It can be pretty overwhelming, so don't be afraid to let your sponsor or therapist know how you are feeling while writing your inventory. As you transfer your story to paper, you are also transferring the pain, guilt and shame onto paper. Writing an inventory can be a very positive transforming experience, and it is vital to your recovery.

Of Ourselves. Once again, you can see this is plural. You can know that others have done this before. You can survive the pain of writing your inventory down. It is joyous to see others freed from their shame. As you see other members of your support groups complete their inventories, you will begin to believe that this release from shame can happen for you too. You are reminded that only you can do this for your- self. Only you know your pain, the strength of your fears, your deepest secrets. Only you are qualified to write this inventory. Now is the time to decide for yourself who you are, and who you want to be. There is great freedom in taking your focus off what is wrong with others, and doing a searching and fearless moral inventory of yourself. You may not understand the value of this step until you have completed it, but it is well worth the pain and tears.

Step Five: *Admitted to God, to ourselves, and to another human being the exact nature of our wrongs.*

Admitted. Here you are again, looking at that word, "admitted." You already know that it means to "fess up," or acknowledge what is already true. You may have already experienced the pain and joy of doing this, probably as a child or adolescent. Perhaps you put yourself in a situation you knew your parents would not approve, or did something wrong, and knew you were going to have to tell them, because you knew they were going to find out anyway. Do you remember your feelings of guilt and shame, like you had let yourself and them down? Then you somehow got the courage to tell them what you had done. You admitted the truth—no matter the consequences. It felt better, finally, to let the secret out.

The same is true in Step Five. You admit all that you have written in your Fourth Step. You let out all those secrets and finally feel that clean joy which comes from truly being totally known.

To God. God might be the easiest person to tell, or the hardest, depending on your relationship with Him. If you feel God has let you down before, admitting what has been wrong in your life can be particularly difficult. Fortunately, God is forgiving of all that you have done, and is willing to restore any lost part of yourself. As one wise person in recovery stated, "It's okay to tell God. God already knows it all anyway, and is just waiting for us to be honest about it too."

To Ourselves. Admitting your past secrets to yourself often takes place as you write your Fourth Step, if you are truly fearless and thorough when writing it. Admitting your powerlessness, your need to be restored to sanity, your profound amazement at your poor choices, and your sincere sense of having failed yourself is probably the most humbling experience you will have with regard to your sense of who you are.

It is at this point, though, that the recovery of your true self is able to take an upward turn, without the overwhelming sense of shame or guilt that has been so closely bound to you in the past. You are now able to begin a more shame-free life, which empowers you to experience the next and most essential part of this step: being able to reveal yourself to another human being.

And to Another Human Being. "What? I have to tell all this stuff to somebody else, face to face?" Yes, telling your story to another human being is the most crucial part of your recovery. In writing your Fourth Step, you have taken your total history of shame, hurt, abandonment, abuse and poor choices, and poured it consciously into one place. Your Fourth Step may even have brought to your conscious awareness some things you have been suppressing for years, and now all of these memories are in one place. If all this pain is kept inside you, and is not shared with another human being, you may talk yourself into believing once again that you are unlovable or unacceptable with such a painful, messy past. You could use this negative information and history for condemnation instead of healing. That is why we must tell another person. We must realize that we are loved and accepted even though we have been places and experienced things of which we are not proud.

In this Fifth Step you experience spiritually, emotionally, and often physically, a cleansing or a lightening of your load. As you share who you have been and what you have experienced with another trusted person, you are reassured that nothing you have done makes you unlovable. Now someone knows the whole truth, and still loves you. It is remarkable!

A note of caution is appropriate here: When you choose someone to hear your Fifth Step, it is important to pick the least condemning, most loving and accepting person you know. You might choose a therapist, sponsor or spiritual person you trust. Choose someone who understands that you are digging into your past in order to make your present and future better—someone who will not shame you for your past. This person can be a member of your support group as well. This choice is yours. Make it in your best interest.

The Exact Nature of Our Wrongs. Fact: this part of the step is very detailed. Two kinds of thought patterns will be addressed. First, those who say, "I can't be specific so I'll never really feel loved," and, second, those who believe that they can own everybody else's wrongs and avoid looking at their own choices. The first person needs to be specific in sharing their story, because the shame they experience about the past is tied to a certain episode. We must talk about those episodes to relieve the shame associated with them. The second person needs to acknowledge their own shortcomings and "clean their own side of the street"—not anyone else's—so that they too can be freed from their own shame.

It's a recognized fact that you can't free anyone else from their shame. Each person has to work their own program of recovery in order to have the kind of happy and fulfilling life we are all capable of experiencing. As a note of caution, for those who have violated children, most states demand professionals report if the specific name and place of this event is given to them. In sharing this information,n be aware of this when doing your Fifth Step.

Step Six: Were entirely ready to have God remove all these defects of character.

Were Entirely Ready. As you move from Step One through Step Five, you discover a process through which you recognize powerlessness, find a God of your understanding, go inside yourself by writing an inventory, and let someone else know who you really are. The very core of the program is in the first five steps. By working these steps you have learned to "trust God and clean house."

Now that you have cleaned house, you must learn how to maintain your new surroundings. It is one process to clean a dirty house, whether you got it dirty yourself or just inherited all the mess—and it is another thing entirely to make sure that it never gets dirty again. That is what Step Six and the following steps are all about—preventative maintenance.

You start by "being entirely ready." This simply means that you are 100 percent ready to look at the damage that was done by all that trash, and you evaluate what you can throw away. You might be quite attached to some of that stuff. Even though it doesn't work any longer, you hesitate to give it up. Someday, some of those old behaviors might come in handy, you keep thinking. You forget that each time you try old behavior it causes great pain. *Were entirely ready* indicates that you are finally tired of the pain. You finally realize that changing is not quite as frightening as staying the same.

To Have God. Having God in our lives is so significant for intimacy anorexics. Here, in Step Six, they are reminded that they, like everyone, are blessed by having a relationship with God. They are beginning to believe that God does want the best for them, and that God wants their lives to express this new way of feeling and believing about themselves. God is willing to work with you, as you continue your efforts at recovery.

Remove All. This sounds like an unrealistic, maybe even painful statement, at least from a human standpoint. "Remove" indicates loss. Intimacy anorexics have certainly experienced loss in their lives. But to lose, or remove, all of their defects? How?

Well, it isn't up to you to decide how; it's only up to you to be ready. Remember that earlier you recognized that you don't have a whole lot of power of your own. In Step Six you will rely on God to have the power to change you—the power you've been unable to access in your addiction.

Defects Of Character. As you consider the phrase, "defects of character," you might be thinking of some of the ways you have behaved and felt that didn't work very well. Go ahead and get a pencil and paper and write down what comes to mind. Reviewing your inventory should give you a good idea of things about your character you might want to change.

For example, perhaps the way you express your anger indicates a defect of character. Maybe the way you control, manipulate your spouse or children, pout to get your own way, isolate or run away from responsibility, are things you want to change. Honesty is important in listing these defects, because the ones you hold on to will keep you stuck in old patterns, and you will continue to attract unhealthy people into your life, especially in intimate relationships.

It is the experience of recovering intimacy anorexics, that as they become healthier and honest, they gravitate toward more healthy and honest people, and are better able to determine who is unhealthy. Understanding this can certainly motivate you to really look at your defects of character, and be 100 percent willing to have God remove them. This is the real release that prevents the dust and trash from resettling in your house.

Step Seven: Humbly asked God to remove our shortcomings.

Humbly. Many struggle with the word, "humble," having been humiliated time and again.

Humility is not the same as humiliation, although you may feel something like humiliation as you see the devastation in your own life and the lives of those around you caused by your defects of character. Humility, in this case, means recognizing your true humanness. You see in Step Seven the manner with which you should approach God. Humility means knowing that you don't have the power to change yourself, but that God does. You come into God's presence with a humble heart, but with hope as well. And as you ask, you shall receive. As long as you don't have preconceived ideas of just how and when God will remove your defects of character, you will have them removed.

Asked God. Humility requires that we ask, not tell, God anything. By now, perhaps you have come to believe that God really does want the best for you, wants you to be free of your defects of character, wants you to feel good about yourself, and to be attracted to healthy people. You are asking, in a sense, to do God's will.

To Remove Our Shortcomings. In Step Six you became ready. Now you push the "go" button, and ask God to take your defects of character or shortcomings. It would be nice if it happened all at once, but again you will experience it as a process. In this process, God will be with you throughout your life, removing your shortcomings as you continue to identify them when they surface, as long as you are willing to ask for help.

For some anorexics, this step comes easily. For others, it is very hard, especially if you are holding on, still rationalizing, still defending, and still gripping your defense mechanisms. In that case, Step Seven can be a painful experience. As someone once said in a meeting, "There was never anything I let go of that didn't have claw marks all over it, including my defects of character."

You can trust that if you ask, God will remove your defects of character, no matter how much you resist. If you decide to hold on to them, you will be fighting a losing battle. It is at this point that you will really need your support group. They will give you valuable feedback about any shortcomings they see you holding on to. If you aren't sure, ask questions. They will also give you support as you try new behaviors, in place of the old ones, that kept you so unhappy. Allow them to support you in this growth process.

Step Eight: Made a list of all persons we had harmed, and became willing to make amends to them all.

Made A List. You probably don't have any problem shopping for groceries if you've made a list. You know that the most efficient way to shop is to have a written list, instead of just mental notes, because otherwise you are likely to get home and find you have forgotten some essential items. There is a saying in Alcoholics Anonymous that you should be fearless and thorough from the very start. This is true in Step Eight. Again, take a pencil and paper in hand, and looking at your inventory, make a list of all those you have harmed. This list should include yourself as well as others, and can also include what damage was done, and the person's name.

Of All Persons. Here again is that sometimes scary word: *all.* "All" means every single one. You are, once again, being challenged to be honest. To the degree that you can be honest in making this list, you will have hope for new relationships with important people in your life.

We Had Harmed. It takes an honest person to look at their life and see the people they have harmed. It is often easier to see how you have been harmed by others. In Steps Four and Five, you looked at how you have been hurt by trusted people in your life, how you have been traumatized, how you have been emotionally abandoned, and how you have suffered. But, if all you look at is how you have been harmed, you are only halfway healed.

Just as it can be painful for a recovering alcoholic to see how their drinking damaged those around them, it can be painful for the recovering intimacy anorexic to realize what he or she has done to hurt others. For many intimacy anorexics, it is much more comfortable to be the victim. As a matter of fact, they have often been the victim of their own behavior, of their own past, and even of recent relationships. But past victimization by others just makes it that much more difficult for these people to realize that they have actually harmed other people. The acting in behavior is just the start of this list. The harm can be very subtle. You need to really search your mind and heart, in order to complete your healing.

And Became Willing. The past tense here reminds you, one more time, that the hard work demanded in the previous steps is survivable. Intimacy anorexics have worked their way through these steps before, and have found peace and happiness on the other side. It also indicates a process. Recovery doesn't just happen overnight. *Becoming willing* takes time, especially if you are holding on to a victim status.

To Make Amends. What does it mean to make amends? For intimacy anorexics, or anyone in recovery for that matter, to make amends means to acknowledge the wrong they have done, and be willing to be different. You stop blaming the other person to justify your own behavior. You stop rationalizing, and defending yourself. You stop avoiding responsibility. You are continuing to change in your relationships with yourself and others. You take full responsibility for what you have done, and to whom you have done it (at least on paper at this point).

To Them All. Here is that word "all" again. It seems to appear everywhere throughout the steps. By now your list should include everyone who has in any way been harmed by your actions or lack of actions. You should have found the willingness to be different with each person on that list, including yourself. No stone should be left unturned at this point, or you will still carry old guilt that will keep you stuck in old sick patterns of thinking and relating. With names, phone numbers, and accounts of damages in hand, you are ready to move on.

Step Nine: *Made direct amends to such people wherever possible, except when to do so would injure them or others.*

Made Direct Amends. In Step Eight, you made your list. Now you go to the grocery store. In Step Nine, you actually go to the people on your list and make direct amends to them for the inappropriate attitudes or behaviors you have had in the past that have affected them. Notice again that this step is written in the past tense. These steps were written in the late 1930s when the first members of Alcoholics Anonymous became sober. Working these steps, especially Step Nine, was something they had to do to maintain their sobriety, so they would not have to carry the pain, shame or guilt of the past or present into their new, sober lives.

They had to be honest with themselves. Be honest as you go to each person on your list and ask them for their forgiveness. When you acknowledge how your behavior affected your relationships with them, you will find the most incredible freedom. Tremendous emotional weights can be lifted, and often relationships can be restored, as the result of working Step Nine. This is not a 100 percent guarantee, since some relationships will remain fractured. However, at least your side of the street will be clean.

You will begin to feel wholeness and happiness in your life, now that you have made the effort to vent completely, without expectations. This is a significant point: You do not make amends with the expectation that your friends or family will change their behavior. You do not make amends with the expectation that people will respond in any certain way. People may, in fact, respond when you make amends, but it is by no means the motivation for you to do what you must to get rid of what you have been carrying for so long. Inflated expectations can cause you much pain, because others are not always in the same place with their recovery that you are with yours. Many people do not choose a path of recovery at all. Your personal efforts and behavior can challenge them into this kind of recovery at some point in the future.

It is not a given that the other person will ask forgiveness in return, even though they may have injured you much more than you have injured them. Your goal is to clean your own slate. You are not responsible for what others leave undone, nor can their shortcomings keep you from recovering and feeling good about yourself.

Except When To Do So Would Injure Them or Others. When you get to this point, you may become confused when you attempt to decide if making amends will injure the person involved, or be detrimental to other, possibly innocent people. Such confusion is best resolved with the assistance of a group, sponsor or therapist. Confusion is not to be used, however, as an excuse to not make any amends because you don't want to experience the pain or shame of admitting your past behavior.

What you must consider, when admitting past behavior is whether or not your confession would significantly damage the other person involved. In this case, you should not raise the issue to them. You can ask yourself, "Would this be damaging?" If you have a question, do not assume you have the answer. You could very possibly avoid an amend which could restore a relationship, or hold on to an amend that will set you up for old behavior. Go over your list with a sponsor, support group or therapist if at all possible.

Step Ten: *Continued to take personal inventory and when we were wrong, promptly admitted it.*

Continued. Here again, you must deal with the maintenance of your newly clean house. You are not letting the dust fall. You are not letting the dirt collect, or the garbage overflow in the can. Here you are in a process, as in Steps Four and Five. Today, when you have been inappropriate or have violated anyone's boundaries, including your own, you don't have to wait five or ten years to make amends. You can do it as you go along.

To Take Personal Inventory. Taking a daily, personal inventory is a process in which intimacy anorexics are able to look at each person in their life, and see how they are interacting with this person. They look at their attitudes toward others and honestly evaluate them. This is not done to the point where they are unable to enjoy interactions, but it is an honest evaluation of how they respond to peers, family, and in all other relationships. It also is a reminder that you inventory only your own behavior, not anyone else's.

And When We Were Wrong, Promptly Admitted It. You will be wrong. This part of Step Ten says, "When" not "If" you were wrong. Many intimacy anorexics have been wronged, but there will still be times when you will be wrong yourself. It is so important for the recovering person to stay free, and not enter into a place of guilt and shame, which can push you into some acting in behavior. So, in the maintenance of Step Ten, when you are wrong, you promptly admit it. "Promptly" is significant because it keeps you from holding on to the baggage, thinking for months about whether you were or weren't wrong. "Promptly" means admit it right now, right here. If you have been acting inappropriately, say, "I'm sorry. Forgive me; I'm acting inappropriately." It is as simple as that. Step Ten gives you a way to stay free from the bondage of guilt and shame. It keeps you humble, which often helps you to remain healthy.

Step Eleven: *Sought through prayer and meditation to improve our conscious contact with God as we understood God, praying only for knowledge of God's will for us and the power to carry that out.*

Sought Through Prayer and Meditation. This step not only tells you what you are doing, but it also tells you how to do it. You are seeking. You are looking to improve your relationship with God. This step tells you to do that through prayer and meditation. Prayer is that verbal, and sometimes internal, communication with God. It is such a positive experience for the intimacy anorexic to become more aware of God in their life. This step lets you know that it is your responsibility. Seeking requires action on your part. You may have felt abandoned by God, since you put no real effort into trying to find out where He was. It has been said many times in meetings, "If you can't find God, guess who moved." You move away from God, God never moves away from you. Seeking Him is all that it takes to find Him.

Meditation is a sometimes a deeper sense of prayer. Prayer is requesting, asking, interacting. Meditation is listening and hearing God's voice. A lot of humans experience rest and peace through meditation, and are able to still the constant obsessive thinking that prevents them from hearing what God has to say. They hear that they are significant, loved, and they deserve to be healthy. Meditate on God's character, on your personal relationship with Him, on some scripture or recovery material you have, and allow them to really sink in to your spirit. Be still, and God will speak to you.

To Improve Our Conscious Contact With God. Most intimacy anorexics, like many people, have an unconscious contact with God. They rely most of the time on their own thinking and resources, and connect with God only after they have thoroughly botched their lives. Step Eleven reminds you to keep God in your conscious mind. You are then able to experience the power and love of God in a whole new way.

As a result, you will experience life in a whole new way. You will have a higher sense of purpose and joy. The result of this new awareness of God on a moment to moment basis is a better relationship with God. As with any relationship, efforts at improving the relationship require time, energy, and some sort of communication. With time, you will find the method of communication that works best for you. There is no right or wrong way to do it. Just do it.

As We Understood God. It is impossible for any one of us to totally understand God. Indeed, my understanding of God might not work for you, nor yours for me. The beauty of the program is that you can begin to see evidence of God in other people. Remember, this is not a job you undertake on your own. You come to a new understanding of God as you interact with the people in your support group, church, or other community of people, seeking knowledge of God. As you listen, you will grow in understanding through other people's experiences of God in their lives.

Praying Only For Knowledge of God's Will For Us. By now, you are beginning to see the benefits of letting go of self will. In Step Eleven, you are gently reminded that when you pray for God's will in your life, you are asking for the absolute best solution to whatever you are facing. So often we push and push situations to turn out the way we want them to, only to find out that we got second or third or seventh or tenth best. It is a very positive thing to realize that you can trust God to have your best interests at heart. The people, places and things you have given your will over to in the past did not have your best interests at heart. You now trust God enough to say, "Not my will, but thy will be done."

And The Power to Carry That Out. You pray for knowledge of God's will, not just for the sake of having the information, but also for the power to carry it out. Having the information without the willingness or power to carry it out, will not change anything. After prayer for the knowledge, you can now listen in meditation for God to tell you the things you need to do. Sometimes a path will open, sometimes God will bring to mind a defect of character that is getting in your way, and sometimes God will challenge you in the way you are behaving through intuitive thoughts or feelings you may have. Often the power to make the changes God seems to want you to make comes through the people in your support groups. It can even come from seeing someone stuck in old behaviors. You can be motivated to change, by seeing the consequences others are experiencing, because of their unwillingness to act differently. Once, having asked for direction and listened for guidance, you can act with assurance, knowing that if you are on the wrong track, you will come to know it. And you always know that you're not alone.

Step Twelve: *Having had a spiritual awakening as the result of these steps, we tried to carry this message to others and to practice these principles in all our day-to-day living.*

Having Had A Spiritual Awakening As The Result Of These Steps. It is no wonder that an individual who comes to the steps-(and in the process of time admits to powerlessness) admits to humanness, admits to the need for a relationship with God, actively pursues that relationship, cleans house, makes amends, and maintains this behavior—has a spiritual awakening. This spiritual awakening is the purpose of working the steps. It is an awakening in which the intimacy anorexic discovers they have worth and value. They are loved by God and can be loved by others, if they will only believe in their lovableness and open up their heart and let that love in.

This awakening to a spiritual connection with God can give the addict the power to change their way of relating to themselves and the world. They can now see themselves as a precious child of a loving God, and treat themselves and others accordingly.

We Tried to Carry This Message to Others. In the beginning of Alcoholics Anonymous, it was not a matter of a drunk alcoholic seeking advice and support from someone who was sober. It was the recovering alcoholic who sought out the active drinker. Bill W., the cofounder of AA, knew that if he couldn't share what he had discovered about his relationship with God and its importance to his sobriety, he wouldn't be able to stay sober. This is true for intimacy anorexics too. As you progress in your recovery, and become less absorbed in your own pain, you begin to recognize when others around you are in pain. You will begin to see opportunities to share your experience, strength, and hope with other intimacy anorexics who are suffering from the same low self esteem, dependency or independency problems, and lack of boundaries that you experienced. You will share, not to get them well, but remain mindful of the miracle of recovery in your own life. Without constant reminders, you are likely to forget where your strength and health come from, and become complacent.

One of the truest sayings around recovery groups is, "You can't keep it if you don't give it away." The door to recovery is opened to you because others passed this way before. It is your joy, as well as your responsibility, to keep the door open for those who follow you, and lead them to the door if they can't find it. It is the only way to ensure freedom for all.

And To Practice These Principles In All Our Day-To-Day Living. Here is the most practical part of the Twelve-Steps. Take what you have learned, and keep doing it every day. Practice admitting your powerlessness over the problems in your life. Practice acknowledging God's ability to run your life and keep you from practicing old behaviors. Practice new thinking and behavior skills. Practice prayer and meditation. Like the athlete who must exercise daily to stay in shape, you need to practice daily the new skills you have learned, so you can stay in good emotional and spiritual shape. It took many years of practicing old behaviors for you to end up in an anorexic lifestyle. It will take practice to become the new person you want to be. But it is possible!

Congratulations to all who embark on this journey of the Twelve-Steps. These steps, when followed, are a tried and true path to recovery from the addiction to withholding that is killing your marriage.

Intimacy Anorexia: The Book

Appendix

Intimacy Anorexia: The Book

FEELINGS EXERCISE

1. I feel (put feeling word here) when (put a present situation).
2. I first remember feeling (put the same feeling word here) when (explain earliest occurrence of this feeling).

Abandoned	Argumen-	Burdened	Coy	Dirty
Abused	tative	Burned	Crabby	Disenchanted
Aching	Aroused	Callous	Cranky	Disgusted
Accepted	Astonished	Calm	Crazy	Disinterested
Accused	Assertive	Capable	Creative	Dispirited
Accepting	Attached	Captivated	Critical	Distressed
Admired	Attacked	Carefree	Criticized	Distrustful
Adored	Attentive	Careful	Cross	Distrusted
Adventurous	Attractive	Careless	Crushed	Disturbed
Affectionate	Aware	Caring	Cuddly	Dominated
Agony	Awestruck	Cautious	Curious	Domineering
Alienated	Badgered	Certain	Cut	Doomed
Aloof	Baited	Chased	Damned	Doubtful
Aggravated	Bashful	Cheated	Dangerous	Dreadful
Agreeable	Battered	Cheerful	Daring	Eager
Aggressive	Beaten	Childlike	Dead	Ecstatic
Alive	Beautiful	Choked Up	Deceived	Edgy
Alone	Belligerent	Close	Deceptive	Edified
Alluring	Belittled	Cold	Defensive	Elated
Amazed	Bereaved	Comfortable	Delicate	Embarrassed
Amused	Betrayed	Comforted	Delighted	Empowered
Angry	Bewildered	Competent	Demeaned	Empty
Anguished	Blamed	Competitive	Demoralized	Enraged
Annoyed	Blaming	Complacent	Dependent	Enraptured
Anxious	Bonded	Complete	Depressed	Enthusiastic
Apart	Bored	Confident	Deprived	Enticed
Apathetic	Bothered	Confused	Deserted	Esteemed
Apologetic	Brave	Considerate	Desirable	Exasperated
Appreciated	Breathless	Consumed	Desired	Excited
Appreciative	Bristling	Content	Despair	Exhilarated
Apprehensive	Broken-up	Cool	Despondent	Exposed
Appropriate	Bruised	Courageous	Destroyed	Fake
Approved	Bubbly	Courteous	Different	

Fascinated	Joyous	Paralyzed	Repulsive
Feisty	Lively	Paranoid	Resentful
Ferocious	Lonely	Patient	Resistant
Foolish	Loose	Peaceful	Responsible
Forced	Lost	Pensive	Responsive
Forceful	Loving	Perceptive	Repressed
Forgiven	Low	Perturbed	Respected
Forgotten	Lucky	Phony	Restless
Free	Lustful	Pleasant	Revolved
Friendly	Mad	Pleased	Riled
Frightened	Maudlin	Positive	Rotten
Frustrated	Malicious	Powerless	Ruined
Full	Mean	Present	Sad
Funny	Miserable	Precious	Safe
Furious	Misunder-	Pressured	Satiated
Gay	stood	Pretty	Satisfied
Generous	Moody	Proud	Scared
Grouchy	Morose	Pulled apart	Scolded
Grumpy	Mournful	Put down	Scorned
Hard	Mystified	Puzzled	Scrutinized
Harried	Nasty	Quarrelsome	Secure
Hassled	Nervous	Queer	Seduced
Healthy	Nice	Quiet	Seductive
Helpful	Numb	Raped	Self-centered
Helpless	Nurtured	Ravished	Self-con-
Hesitant	Nuts	Ravishing	scious
High	Obsessed	Real	Selfish
Hollow	Offended	Refreshed	Separated
Honest	Open	Regretful	Sensuous
Hopeful	Ornery	Rejected	Sexy
Hopeless	Out of	Rejuvenated	Shattered
Horrified	control	Rejecting	Shocked
Hostile	Overcome	Relaxed	Shot down
Humiliated	Overjoyed	Relieved	Shy
Hurried	Overpowered	Remarkable	Sickened
Hurt	Overwhelmed	Remembered	Silly
Hyper	Pampered	Removed	Sincere
Ignorant	Panicked	Repulsed	Sinking

Smart
Smothered
Smug
Sneaky
Snowed
Soft
Solid
Solitary
Sorry
Spacey
Special
Spiteful
Spontaneous
Squelched
Starved
Stiff
Stimulated
Stifled
Strangled
Strong
Stubborn
Stuck
Stunned
Stupid
Subdued
Submissive
Successful
Suffocated
Sure
Sweet
Sympathy
Tainted
Tearful
Tender
Tense
Terrific
Terrified
Thrilled

Ticked
Tickled
Tight
Timid
Tired
Tolerant
Tormented
Torn
Tortured
Touched
Trapped
Tremendous
Tricked
Trusted
Trustful
Trusting
Ugly
Unacceptable
Unapproachable
Unaware
Uncertain
Uncomfortable
Under control
Understanding
Understood
Undesirable
Unfriendly
Ungrateful
Unified
Unhappy
Unimpressed
Unsafe
Unstable
Upset
Uptight
Used
Useful
Useless

Unworthy
Validated
Valuable
Valued
Victorious
Violated
Violent
Voluptuous
Vulnerable
Warm
Wary
Weak
Whipped
Whole
Wicked
Wild
Willing
Wiped out
Wishful
Withdrawn
Wonderful
Worried
Worthy

Guideline #1: No Examples about
Each Other
Guideline #2: Maintain Eye Contact
Guideline #3: No Feedback

Intimacy Anorexia Groups

What are Intimacy Anorexia Groups?

Intimacy Anorexia Groups are support groups for people desiring to be free from withholding toward their spouse.

How Do They Work?

Anyone willing to start an Intimacy Anorexia group can do so. Intimacy Anorexia Groups are work groups. Group members are expected to do the work in Intimacy Anorexia: The Workbook, Intimacy Anorexia: The Steps, keep the 5 commandments and do the Three Dailies with their spouse. Below are some guidelines for starting and maintaining an Intimacy Anorexia group.

Intimacy Anorexia Group Roles

1. The pointperson serves as the contact person for new members to be brought into the group. This is to protect the group from someone just dropping in on the group. The pointperson can serve for an indefinite amount of time but should be reconsidered after one year of service.

2. The chairperson of the meeting is responsible to start the meeting by asking the pointperson if there are any new people. The chairperson starts the introductions and selects the topic for group discussion. The chairperson serves the group for a maximum of 8 weeks. At that time, someone else volunteers.

Intimacy Anorexia Meetings

1. New Members: Any new members are introduced by the pointperson and are asked to verbalize their anorexic behaviors and their desire to have sobriety from these behaviors.

2. Introductions: Beginning with the chairperson of the meeting, introductions are completed as follows: The chairperson introduces themselves, shares their feelings, shares their boundaries and length of time free from those behaviors.

Example: "My name is John/Jane. I feel "alone" and "anticipation." My boundaries are no withholding through anger, criticism and limiting sex or praise from my spouse. I worked on Exercise #12-19 this week in the Intimacy Anorexia workbook and made four pages of progress in my Anorexia step workbook. I have done my Three Dailies with my spouse, 7 days out of 7 days this week and I have been sober for 39 days."

3. Discussion: The chairperson chooses a topic related to staying free from Intimacy Anorexia which the group discusses. Each member can share without feedback from the group unless feedback is specifically requested by that member.

4. Honest Time: Group members break off into 2-3 members and discuss thoughts, behaviors, struggles and successes since the last meeting specfically about anorexic behavior toward their spouse.

5. Closing Prayer: Group members come back together and repeat the Lord's Prayer as a group.

5 Commandments For the first 100 Days of Recovery:

1. Pray in the morning, asking God to keep you giving toward your spouse today.

2. Read Intimacy related materials.

3. Call someone in your group and check in with that person during the day.

4. Meetings, attend every meeting possible.

5. Pray in the evening, thanking God for keeping you free from Intimacy Anorexia today.

3 Dailies

1. Two Feelings - Daily share two of your feelings from that day with your spouse.

2. Two Praises - Daily share with your spouse two positive things about them.

3. Pray - Daily pray out loud with your spouse.

Consequence: Set a consequence if you do not initiate the 3 Dailies with your spouse daily or if you are withholding sexually from your spouse.

Support Groups

Sex Addiction

Sex Addicts
Anonymous (SAA)
(713) 869-4902
www.saa-recovery.org

Sexaholics Anon.
(866) 424-8777
www.sa.org

Sexual Compulsives
Anonymous (SCA)
1-800-977-HEAL
www.sca-recovery.org

Sex & Love Addicts
Anon.
210-828-7900
www.slaafws.org

Sexual Recovery
Anonymous (SRA),
(212) 340-4650 or:
Canada
(604) 290-9382
www.sexualrecovery.org

Freedom Groups
*Faith-Based for
Sex Addicts*
(719) 278-3708
www.sexaddict.com

For the Partner or Family Member

COSA
(612) 537-6904
www.cosa-recovery.org

S-Anon Intrntnl.
Family Groups
(615) 833-3152
www.sanon.org

Co-SLAA
www.coslaa.org

Partners Groups
(719) 278-3708
www.sexaddict.com

Recovering Couples
Anonymous (RCA)
(510) 663-2312
www.recovering-
couples.org

Sexual Trauma Survivors

Survivors of Incest
Anonymous (SIA)
(410) 282-3400
www.siawso.org

Incest Survivors Anon.
P.O. Box 17245
Long Beach, CA 90807
(562) 428-5599

Sexual Assault Recov.
Anonymous
Canada (604) 584-2626
www.r-a.org

The Twelve Steps of Alcoholics Anonymous
Adapted for Intimacy Anorexics

1. We admitted we were powerless over our intimacy anorexia-that our lives had become unmanageable.

2. Came to believe that a Power greater than ourselves could restore us to sanity.

3. Made a decision to turn our will and our lives over to the care of God as we understood Him.

4. Made a searching and fearless moral inventory of ourselves.

5. Admitted to God, to ourselves, and to another human being the exact nature of our wrongs.

6. Were entirely ready to have God remove all these defects of character.

7. Humbly asked Him to remove our shortcomings.

8. Made a list of all people we had harmed, and became willing to make amends to them all.

9. Made direct amends to such people wherever possible, except when to do so would injure them or others.

10. Continued to take personal inventory, and when we were wrong, promptly admitted it.

11. Sought through prayer and meditation to improve our conscious contact with God as we understood Him, praying only for knowledge of His will for us and the power to carry that out.

12. Having had a spiritual awakening as the result of these steps, we tried to carry this message to others and to practice these principles in all our affairs.

Resources by Dr. Weiss

Intimacy Anorexia Recovery

Intimacy Anorexia (DVD—$69.95)
This DVD explains the age old question, "Why doesn't my partner want to be intimacy with me?" It includes 90 minutes of up-to-date information on sexual, emotional and spiritual anorexia and can open new insights for individuals or couples to begin a life of intimacy. This DVD will give you the characteristics, causes and strategies of intimacy anorexia. This DVD also provides solutions for the intimacy anorexic to start their road to recovery.

Married and Alone (DVD—$49.95)
This DVD is for the spouse of an intimacy/sexual anorexic. You feel disconnected, untouched and often unloved. You are not crazy and Dr. Weiss will help you to start a journey of recovery from living with a spouse with intimacy/sexual anorexia.

Intimacy Anorexia-The Book (Book—$22.95)
This is the first book to address intimacy anorexia. Regardless if you are the anorexic or the spouse you will learn the characteristics, strategies and patterns of intimacy anorexia. You will also be introduced to why intimacy anorexia is an addiction as well as the beginning steps to recovery for the intimacy anorexic

Intimacy Anorexia-The Workbook (Workbook—$39.95)
This is like therapy in a box. You will be exposed to over 100 exercises that have already been proven helpful in Dr. Weiss' practice of treating intimacy anorexia step by step the anorexia is taken from withholding intimacy to be able to give intimacy if they do these crucial exercises

Intimacy Anorexia-The Steps (Workbook—$14.95)
The twelve steps have helped millions heal from many types of addiction. This si the only twelve step workbook just for intimacy anorexia. Each step give you progress in you healing from intimacy anorexia.

Intimacy Anorexia for Christians (DVD—$49.95)
In this DVD Christians are exposed to Biblical principles for paradigming intimacy anorexia. This DVD also engages Biblical resources for the Christian intimacy anorexia to overcome intimacy anorexia in their lives and motivate them to give their heart to their spouse.

Marriage

The Ten-Minute Marriage Principle (Book—$14.99)
By taking just ten minutes a day to focus on each other, you can enhance your marriage in ways you'll appreciate for a lifetime. As you and your spouse learn to talk and understand each other more fully, you'll ignite true, lasting intimacy.

Intimacy: A 100 Day Guide to Lasting Relationships (Book—$11.99)
Dr. Weiss walks couples through the skills necessary for lifelong intimate relationships. This guide can transform couples to deeper levels of intimacy.

The 7 Love Agreements (Book—$13.99, DVD $12.95)
These seven agreements are so powerful only one person needs to apply them to see a marriage make progress. Weiss explains the power of agreement in the areas of faithfulness, patience, forgiveness, service, respect, kindness and celebration. Weiss encourages men and women to grow closer to their spouse by entering mutually beneficial agreements, individually or as a couple.

Winning @ Marriage (DVD—$69.00)
This three-DVD, 4 1/2 hour marriage conference is for everybody. You will gain insight, laugh and most importantly walk through the practical tools to make your marriage a winning marriage.

The Best Sex of Your Life, For Men or Women (DVD—$29.95 Each)
This video is a must for every Christian man or woman. You are practically and passionately walked through Christian sexuality that really works. For over a decade, couples have been using these principles and techniques to radically improve their love life.

How to Really Love a Woman (DVD—$69.00)

In this 12 part DVD series, you will be exposed to tried and true principles to help you learn how to really love a woman. These 30 minute sessions are easily and immediately applicable. Begin to love your spouse the way you wished you could. Dr. Weiss' practical tools will make you more successful at loving your spouse.

Women's Recovery

Partners: Healing from his Addiction (Book—$14.95)

This book has the latest research on the effects to partners of sex addicts. Riveting statistics are combined with personal stories of partners in recovery.

Partner's Recovery Guide: 100 Empowering Exercises (Workbook—$39.95)

This is the most practical workbook for partners and was conceived from many years of successful treatment for partners of sex addicts. It includes 100 proven techniques used in counseling sessions to help partners.

Beyond Love: 12-Step Recovery Guide for Partners (Workbook—$14.95)

This is an interactive workbook that allows the partner to gain insight and strength through working the Twelve Steps. This book can be used individually or as a group step-study workbook.

Now That I Know, What Should I Do? (DVD—$69.00)

This DVD answers the ten most frequently asked questions by partners who have just found out about their spouse's sexual addiction. The need for counseling is significantly reduced by listening to this video.

Partner to Partner (DVD—$19.95)

This DVD is a dialogue of several partners of sex addicts sharing their hope and experience. These women address key issues facing a partner of a sex addict and their journey through recovery.

Men's Recovery

The Final Freedom (Book—$22.95, CD—$35.00)
Plentiful, current information on sexual addiction and recovery that goes beyond what many counselors can offer. Many attest to successful recovery from this product alone.

101 Freedom Exercises for Sexual Addiction Recovery (Workbook—$39.95)
Proven techniques Dr. Weiss has recommended through the years to successfully help thousands gain and maintain recovery from sexual addiction. A Christian Edition of 101 Practical Exercises

Steps to Freedom: A Christian 12-Step Guide (Workbook—$14.95)
This is a thorough interaction with the Twelve Steps of recovery from a Christian perspective. This workbook can be used in Twelve-Step study groups or for individual use.

Sex, Men and God (Book—$13.99, CD—$29.95)
Finally, an encouraging message for men who want to be sexually successful! God is not against sexual pleasure in your marriage! In fact, He created it! So what is keeping you from experiencing the best of His creation? This book has clearly and creatively outlined practical, doable suggestions and principles that will help you enjoy your sexuality as God intended.

6 Types of Sex Addicts (CD—$29.95)
This CD will give you more information than most therapists have on sexual addiction. You will be able to finally know how you became a sex addict and identify why you might still be relapsing. A must for every sex addict in recovery!

Treatment for the 6 Types of Sex Addicts (CD—$29.95)
This CD will take you to the next level in your recovery. Once you know the type of sex addict you are, Dr. Doug outlines the same treatment plan you would receive in an individual session.

Addict to Addict (DVD—$29.95)
This amazing DVD has 8 addicts telling their stories through directed questions. These individuals address key issues along with their journey through recovery. A must DVD for every sex addict.

Female Addict Recovery

Secret Solutions (Workbook—$39.95)
This is a practical recovery exercise workbook written specifically for female sex addicts. Many of these techniques have been successful to help other female sex addicts. This is the most solution-oriented and practical workbook for female sexual addiction to date.

She has a Secret (e-Book--$11.95)
Twenty-four recovering female sex addicts share their stories of addiction, consequences and their recovery. This book is the most current book in the field of sex addiction for women and is packed with new statistics to further our understanding of female sexual addiction. This is a must read for any woman struggling in this addiction, as well as for professionals in this field. Visit www.sexaddict.com.

Other Resources

Beyond the Bedroom (Book—$14.95)
This is the first book to discuss the issues of adult children of sex addicts, as well as provides a road map to recovery. You will also be exposed to research findings on the impact of being a child of a sexual addict.

Get a Grip: How to Turn Your Worst Behaviors into Strengths (Book—$19.99)
This book will take you from having behaviors control you into learning how to control your behaviors. This book is packed with helpful information for anyone struggling with a behavior that seems to be controlling them. This step-by-step process can help you go from repeat failure to success.

The Power of Pleasure (Book—$14.95, CD—$14.95)
Knowing how you are created for pleasure is pivotal in having happiness. Your pleasure zones and hierarchy are as unique as you are. This book unlocks your ability to have a life full of your pleasures.

ITEM	QUAN	PRICE	TOTAL
Intimacy Anorexia DVD	___	69.95	___
Married and Alone DVD	___	69.95	___
Intimacy Anorexia-The Book	___	69.95	___
Intimacy Anorexia-The Workbook	___	69.95	___
Intimacy Anorexia-The Steps	___	69.95	___
Intimacy Anorexia for Christians	___	69.95	___
The Ten-Minute Marriage Principle	___	69.95	___
Intimacy: A 100 Day Guide	___	69.95	___
The 7 Love Agreements Book	___	69.95	___
The 7 Love Agreements DVD	___	69.95	___
Winning @ Marriage	___	69.95	___
The Best Sex of Your Life for Men Only	___	69.95	___
The Best Sex of Your Life for Women Only	___	69.95	___
How to Really Love a Woman	___	69.95	___
Partners: Healing from His Addiction	___	69.95	___
Partner's Recovery Guide: 100 Emp. Exc.	___	69.95	___
Beyond Love	___	69.95	___
Now That I Know, What Should I Do?	___	69.95	___
Partner to Partner	___	69.95	___
The Final Freedom Book	___	69.95	___
The Final Freedom CD	___	69.95	___
101 Freedom Exercises for Sex Addict. Rec	___	69.95	___
Steps to Freedom	___	69.95	___
Sex, Men and God Book	___	69.95	___
Sex, Men and God CD	___	69.95	___
6 Types of Sex Addicts	___	69.95	___
Treatment for the 6 Types of Sex Addicts	___	69.95	___
Addict to Addict	___	69.95	___
Secret Solutions Workbook	___	69.95	___
Beyond the Bedroom	___	69.95	___
Get a Grip	___	69.95	___
The Power of Pleasure Book	___	69.95	___
The Power of Pleasure CD	___	69.95	___

	Sub Total	___

7.4% Sales Tax (in Colorado only)

Shipping/Handling-add $8 + 1 for each additional item (in USA)   ___

Shipping/Handling-add $30 + $1 for each additional item (outside USA)   ___

Total   ___

To Order: 719-278-3708

VISA/MC/DISCOVER # _____ EXP DATE _____

NAME _____ SIGNATURE _____

ADDRESS _____ CITY _____

STATE _____ ZIP CODE _____ PHONE (_____)_____

MAIL: Heart to Heart Counseling Centers, P.O. Box 51055, Colorado Springs, CO 80949

E-MAIL: heart2heart@xc.org   **Website: www.intimacyanorexia.com**

(Make Checks payable to Heart to Heart Counseling Center)

Telephone   Counseling

Telephone counseling is convenient and effective.

Individual Telephone Counseling - Individual counseling offers a personal treatment plan for successful healing in your life by telephone. A counselor can help you understand how you became stuck and gives strategies for you to begin your road to recovery.

Couple Telephone Counseling - Couples are helped through critical issues in their marriage due to the intimacy anorexia of one or both people in the marriage. We have helped many couples rebuild their relationship, as they begin to understand and implement the necessary skills for an intimate relationship.

Partner Telephone Counseling - Partners of intimacy anorexics need an advocate to call upon. Feelings of fear, hurt, anger, betrayal, and grief require a compassionate, effective response. We provide that expert guidance and direction. We have helped many partners heal from the side effects of living with an intimacy anorexic. A phone appointment today can begin your personal journey toward healing.

Call Heart to Heart Counseling Center at (719) 278-3708 to schedule your telephone appointment today.

3-Day   Intensive

Intimacy Anorexia Couple Intensive

This intensive serves the needs of couples who are struggling with one or both having intimacy anorexia issues. A master's level counselor will address the structural damage, which takes place in most systems. The couple will attain skills and goals in order to count themselves among the many clients who have successfully remained in committed relationships after the awareness of intimacy anorexia. A new beginning is possible with the tools attained from this intensive. This intensive includes one counseling session for him, one session for her and one session for the couple with a licensed counselor each day. Structured assignments are given to work on during your own time. Attendance is encouraged in our office Intimacy Anorexia Groups and Partner's support groups in the evening. The Intimacy Anorexia Couple's 3-Day Intensive held at Heart to Heart Counseling Center in Colorado Springs, Colorado is available most Mondays through Wednesdays. Call to schedule your intensive at (719) 278-3708.

NOTE: If you need to schedule an intensive with Dr. Weiss immediately and cannot wait until the next scheduled appointment, you may be able to schedule an Emergency Intensive. Call to request an Emergency Intensive, which is priced at a higher rate than the others.

Sexual Addiction Couple Intensive

This intensive serves the needs of couples who are trapped within the disease of sex addiction. A master's level counselor will address the structural damage, which takes place in most systems within sexually addictive relationships. The couple will attain skills and goals in order to count themselves among the many clients who have successfully remained in committed relationships after the awareness of sexual addiction. A new beginning is possible with the tools attained from this intensive. This intensive includes one counseling session for the addict, one session for the partner and one session for the couple with a licensed counselor each day. Structured assignments are given to work on during your own time. Attendance is encouraged in our office Freedom Groups and Partner's support groups in the evening. The Sexual Addiction Couple's 3-Day Intensives held at Heart to Heart Counseling Center in Colorado Springs, Colorado is available most

Mondays through Wednesdays. Call to schedule your intensive at (719) 278-3708.

Sexual Addiction Individual Intensive

Those struggling with sex addiction want solutions. This 3-Day intensive focuses on solutions. Some highlights of this intensive will be:

- Discovering the origination of your sexual addiction
- Outlining a definitive plan for your recovery
- Identifying a working plan for deprivation
- Addressing core issues of sexual addiction

This solution-driven intensive can help make recovery smoother and much more attainable. This intensive would include one and a half sessions of individual counseling in the morning and one session of individual counseling in the afternoon. Structured assignments are given to work on during your own time. Attendance is encouraged in our office support groups in the evening. Sexual Addiction 3-Day Intensives held at Heart to Heart Counseling Center in Colorado Springs, Colorado are available most Mondays through Wednesdays.

Partner Intensive

If you are married or living with an intimacy anorexic or sexual addict, there are often residuals to this. The addict's addiction may have left you feeling hurt, betrayed, angry, confused or even hopeless. This 3-Day intensive allows you to look at yourself, as well as the consequences of living with an intimacy anorexic or sexual addict. The skills you will learn can expedite your healing from the consequences of their addiction. You deserve to be all you can for the people in your life. This intensive can help you be your best again.

This solution-driven intensive can help make recovery smoother and much more attainable. This intensive would include one and a half sessions of individual counseling in the morning and one session of individual counseling in the afternoon. Structured assignments are given to work on during your own time. Attendance is encouraged in our office support groups in the evening. Partner 3-Day Intensives held at Heart to Heart Counseling Center in Colorado Springs, Colorado are available most Mondays through Wednesdays.

Adult Child of Sexual Addict Intensive

This 3-Day intensive will help anyone who grew up in a home that was tainted by the colors of a sexual addict. Whether it was your mom or dad, you will be able to practically deal with your anger, hurt, betrayal and other issues involved from living with a sexually addicted parent.

Teenaged Child of a Sexual Addict Intensive

Most of us are aware teens are affected by a parent's sexual addiction. If your adolescent is experiencing symptoms from living with a sexually addicted parent in the past or present there is help. This 3-Day intensive can help teens with emotions, pain, anger and the hurt related to the confusion of living with a sexually addicted parent. Teenaged Child of a Sexual Addict 3-Day Intensives held at Heart to Heart Counseling Center in Colorado Springs, Colorado are available most Mondays through Wednesdays.

Sex Abuse Intensive

This 3-Day intensive addresses the residual affects of sexual abuse, which many sex addicts and partners experienced. This intensive focuses on giving relief of the symptoms due to the sexual abuse. Sex Abuse 3-Day Intensives held at Heart to Heart Counseling Center in Colorado Springs, Colorado are available most Mondays through Wednesdays. Schedule your Intensive Today by calling (719) 278-3708.

American Association for Sex Addiction Therapy

Dr. Weiss has created a 45-hour program to train counselors how to work with sexual addicts and partners of sexual addicts. This DVD/Workbook training set is available for anyone who would like to have more information on treating sexual addiction. Everyone who completes this 45-hour course will receive a certificate of completion. This course is for anyone who has a significant interest in the field of sexual addiction. This course can be taken by anyone who wants to increase their knowledge of sex addiction and partner's recovery.

This course is also part of certifying licensed counselors to become certified as a Sexual Recovery Therapist (SRT). If you or a counselor you know has an interest in treating sexual addicts or their spouses call the phone number below.

For more information or to place an order, please call

(719) 330-2425

or visit www.aasat.org